Odd Tales from
THE
Smithsonian

Smithsonian Institution Press · Washington, D.C.

THE PILOT &
THE LION CUB

Odd Tales from
THE
Smithsonian

PEGGY THOMSON / EDWARDS PARK
Illustrations by Loel Barr

Library of Congress Cataloging-in-Publication Data

Thomson, Peggy,
  The pilot and the lion cub.
  Summary: A collection of stories and anecdotes about the
various exhibits housed in the Smithsonian Institution.
  1. Smithsonian Institution—Anecdotes, facetiae, satire, etc.
[1. Smithsonian Institution—Anecdotes, facetiae, satire, etc.]
I. Park, Edwards. II. Barr, Loel, ill. III. Title.
Q11.S8T48 1986   069′.09753   85-600246
ISBN 0-87474-747-3 (pbk. : alk. paper)

Printed in the United States of America
Designed by Maria Epes

The paper in this book meets the guidelines for permanence and
durability of the Committee on Production Guidelines for Book
Longevity of the Council on Library Resources.

Contents

Preface

A lot of odd and amusing things happen as the august Smithsonian Institution goes about its serious business of pursuing its mandate—the increase and diffusion of knowledge. Collected in this book are some sidelights, anecdotes, offbeat stories, and wry observations on what goes on—sometimes—at the Smithsonian.

What was the Great Brain Contest—and who won it? How was Grant framed? Which First Lady threw out the moose heads and why did she do it? What happened when Arabella went into orbit?

For answers to these and other weighty questions, dip into this book of odd tales and other Smithsoniana.

■

The Pilot and the Lion Cub

Roscoe Turner was his name and airplane racing was his game. He was good at it—witness the RT-14 Meteor at the National Air and Space Museum, which won the prestigious Thompson Trophy in 1938 and '39—and he knew it. He designed his own uniforms, usually a powder blue creation. He waxed his mustache until it tapered to a needle. And, because the Gilmore Oil Company sponsored him, he adopted a lion cub, named it Gilmore, and stashed it in the cockpit beside him when he set out to break speed marks.

There were a couple of Gilmores. When the first one got too big to be called a cub, Roscoe replaced him with another. And pretty soon Gilmore the second reached the age of six

11

months and a size that required his own special seat in the cockpit. Turner fixed him up, nice and comfy, and kept flying with him. Gilmore had his own lion-shaped uniform, and a parachute in case something went wrong. The Humane Society insisted on that.

Between races and appearances, the two fliers used to share hotel rooms. But when Gilmore reached full size, he was grounded. Regretfully, Roscoe Turner packed him off to a zoo. When Gilmore died, at age 25, he was stuffed, and on Turner's death he was given to the Smithsonian.

Gilmore goes on exhibit every once in a while at the big museum, but spends most of his time standing guard at the small exhibits building at the Paul E. Garber Facility at Silver Hill, Maryland, where old airplanes are restored and maintained. A lot of the time, the lion is in mothballs—well, a refrigerated vault—along with Turner's lion-skin flying coat with glass lion's-eye buttons. There's also a walking stick, made for the dashing pilot from a lion's tail, complete with tassel.

■

Tamarin Soap Opera

Gorillas at the National Zoo are notorious soap opera fans, watching their favorites every afternoon on their TV sets.

But their tiny cousins, the golden lion tamarins, often seem to live in the middle of a soap opera.

This nervous little monkey with bright orange fur that sweeps around its face like a lion's mane is sadly endangered in its native Brazil. Its natural habitat is a certain rain forest. Because of development, only patches of this forest remain—and it is now being protected for the tamarins. But at the zoo they have flourished, rearing a colony of more than 200, enough to populate several other zoos as well.

The zoo-bred tamarins offer zoologists a rare chance to observe behavior at close quarters—an intimate scrutiny they would never get in the wild. One scientist spent close to a year watching the brilliant little creatures streaking around their branch-filled enclosures, trilling and whining and chirping at each other. He learned a lot about their home life, including the fact that youngsters need practice as babysitters if they're going to be well-adjusted parents.

It seems there were these twin brothers, M00715 and M00716. When their mother produced a baby brother, they helped her out by lugging him on their backs, sharing food with him and letting him steal it from them. Then along came a female tamarin, M00709, who had also done some babysitting, of a sister, though less of it. Aged 15 months, she was introduced to the twins so she could choose a mate.

She chose 716. He had gone through a spell of dominance, acting more aggressively than 715. But then he'd apparently flipped out, dashing around his cage, bashing into walls and tree branches, finally having to be taken away to recover. He was back to normal by the time he met 709, and though she liked both brothers and huddled and groomed with 715, it was 716 who mated with her. In time she gave birth to M01253.

On her second day of motherhood, 709 showed considerable vexation with the baby on her back. She'd whip around and nip him on the cheek. In its nesting box, little 1253 looked cut up about the face and made "troubled, screeching, rasping noises," according to the human observer (who had become pretty agitated himself).

The father, 716, came to the rescue. Normally, male tamarins begin carrying infants when they're three weeks old. But 716 seems to have recognized the emergency in his family. He got 1253 out of the nesting box and took over carrying duties immediately from 709. He had help from his twin, 715, who quickly volunteered to help out, and between them, the brothers saved the baby's life. The facial cuts were slow to heal because 709 continued to nip 1253 when she nursed him. But within two weeks she started to calm down and her little son pulled through. Later he sired young of his own.

The story, along with similar soap operas, indicates to science that these endangered animals must be kept in family groups so that the young take part in infant care. The hope is that they will do this and succeed at parenting when they are transported back to the wild—where some of them have already been sent.

—

Lindbergh's Grandfather's Dog's Denture

Tucked away in a cabinet belonging to the medical sciences division of the National Museum of American History is Charles Lindbergh's grandfather's dog's upper plate. That nicely made doggie denture just happened to be packed in with a collection of false teeth made by Lindbergh's grandfather, Dr. Charles H. Land of Detroit, a dentist who pioneered in porcelain dentures.

Dr. Land's works are fine indeed, though the most appealing items in the collection are some tiny clay toys—a goose, a pigeon, a deer—which he fashioned at his work bench for his grandson, and the upper plate he fashioned for his dog. The dog dentures, it seems, were Land's contribution to a great turn-of-the-century debate. One school of dental thought championed dentures made with various dents, or pockets, intended to create a suction for holding the dentures in place. Land's school claimed (rightly) that such pockets harmed the mouth, that instead dentures must be made to fit exactly and they would then be held in place by surface tension.

After making a set of perfectly fitting teeth for his terrier, Land took his dog with him to dental society meetings. He'd demonstrate his point by inserting the choppers and then throwing the dog a chunk of beef to eat—with ease and dispatch—before the assembled members.

Charles Lindbergh, on visits to Washington, D.C., several times stopped by the museum to look in on his old toys, in amongst the historic teeth, and to chat about the companionable grandparent, who could fix anything with his hands—including the chewing problems of the family's terrier.

—

The Legend of "Old Moneybags"

For 80 years, generations of visitors to the National Museum of Natural History looked upon the life-size model of *Stegosaurus* with special interest. It was a fixture at the old Dinosaur Hall—a small-headed creature with a high rear end and plates all down its spine. And everyone knew that it was stuffed with shredded dollar bills. Even the most scholarly Smithsonian paleontologist spoke of the papier-mâché model as "Old Moneybags."

In the early 1980s work began on the new Dinosaur Hall—a spectacular exhibit with updated displays of prehistoric life based on 80 years of newly gained knowledge. Among the other changes was a rearrangement of the *Stegosaurus* plates to conform to more modern ideas.

But the visit of three formally dressed men to Old Moneybags had nothing to do with the accuracy of the reproduction. They came from the United States Treasury Department. Producing pocket knives, they probed into obscure flaws in the creature. They picked out bits of the interior stuffing, then whisked the dust off their pinstripes and took off. A little later, the news was telephoned back to the Smithsonian: The stuffing of Old Moneybags wasn't money after all. It was shredded newspaper.

So ends a nice old Smithsonian legend. A pity—but that's the way the paper crumples.

—

Upside-Down Stamp
Celebrated Wrong-Way Flight

In the philately section of the Museum of American History, in a darkened showcase that is illuminated only by bursts of light from a pushbutton device, one of the world's most valuable stamps is on display. It's an airmail, marking the first regularly scheduled airmail flight, on May 15, 1918. And the airplane—a Curtiss "Jenny"—is upside down.

The stamp went on sale two days before the flight was scheduled—one plane to carry mail from Washington to Philadelphia, where another would relay it to New York, while the process was simultaneously repeated from New York to Washington. A stamp collector named Bill Robey went to a Washington post office early on the 13th to get a sheet of stamps and mail off stamped envelopes to his friends with that valuable first-day cancellation.

Robey was handed a sheet of 100 for $24. While he was paying, he saw that the stamps had inverted centers: the planes were upside-down! He said later his heart stood still while he fished the bills out of his wallet and handed them to the clerk. Then he asked to see more sheets. They were normal. At that point he told the clerk what he'd got. The clerk ran to the phone, and Robey lit out fast for his office.

That afternoon postal inspectors called on Robey and tried to bully him into returning the faulty sheets. But Robey knew his rights, guessed the value of his inverted stamps, and stood his ground. He rode the trolleys for three hours, reluctant to reach home before dark. He slept, he later reported, with the stamps under the mattress—on his wife's side.

The flight came off as scheduled—well . . . not quite. The Washington-to-Philadelphia plane showed up to load its mail cargo for the flight. President Wilson showed up in his limousine. The mail showed up in a truck and the canvas sacks were stuffed into the forward cockpit.

Then the pilot, Lt. George Boyle, hopped into the rear cockpit, the ground crew pulled the propeller through, there were shouts of "Switch Off!" and then "Contact!" And nothing happened. Mechanics swarmed over the Jenny for 15 minutes until someone checked the gas. Empty.

That was fixed; and with a roar, the engine started. Boyle zoomed into the air. Only a few people who knew something about flying had misgivings when they saw the plane head south instead of toward Philadelphia. But Boyle had been briefed with the aid of a road map. Couldn't be. . . . But it was. Boyle called up, sheepishly, from Waldorf, Maryland, 20 miles away, where he had landed in a plowed field after following the wrong set of railroad tracks. He'd splintered his prop. The mail with the new stamps and the First Day cancellations was trucked back to Washington, then loaded aboard the Philadelphia train.

So the stamps deserved the flight, and vice versa. And the Smithsonian, conservator of the ludicrous as well as the earth-shaking, has an upside-down stamp—and its story—in safekeeping.

Einstein and the Personality Quiz

A number of curious items can be found in the Dibner Library of rare books and manuscripts at the National Museum of American History. There's a single manuscript page of Charles Darwin's *Origin of Species*. (The manuscript didn't survive in one piece because Darwin cannibalized his pages to write on the backs.) A copy of Madame Marie Curie's doctoral thesis has her name misspelled on the cover. And then there are Albert Einstein's penciled replies to a personality quiz, which a sculptor urged him to complete while she worked on a bust of the great man:

Are your best hours those you spend with folks? *"Nein."*

When you work do you seem to disturb people with your noise? Do you whistle, rattle, shut doors carelessly? *"Nein."*

Do you sit straight and erect? *"Ja."*

Do you walk briskly with upright carriage? *"Nein."*

Possibly baffled by number 43—Could someone get in bed with you without waking you up?—Einstein took the liberty of waffling. *"Weiss nicht."*

■

How Grant Was Framed

The portrait of Ulysses S. Grant in the presidential collection of the National Portrait Gallery stops people, partly because Grant looks as though he had a hangover and partly because of the frame. It's an enormous, dark, heavy, intricately carved piece of Victoriana with the General's battles listed around it and an eagle perched on top. Apparently it was first gilded, then much of the gold was painted out with black.

The portrait hung for decades in a hotel lobby in Saratoga Springs, New York. When the Smithsonian got around to buying it, people figured the asking price was $10,000 for the painting and $40,000 for the frame.

—

No Way to Treat a Nude

The Alice Pike Barney Studio House, on Sheridan Circle in Washington, D.C., is one of the Smithsonian's strangest acquisitions. Mrs. Barney, the wife of a wealthy industrialist, was a free spirit of the Victorian age, an artist of moderate talent (she studied with Whistler) and an art enthusiast with imagination, energy, and (best of all) plenty

of money. Her studio house, now open for visits by appointment, was designed purely as a European salon. It marked her attempt to bring a little of the lively bohemianism that had so charmed her in Paris to the barren pastures of Washington. The place has a gallery for the theatricals she loved to present—written and choreographed and costumed and directed by her. It also, so they say, has ample ghosts for most tastes.

In its basement is a life-size stone statue of a young girl, reclining—and nude. Possibly one of the ghosts emanates from the statue, for it suffered considerable humiliation when it was delivered to the studio house during the high tide of late Victorian prudery.

Alice Barney was in Europe when the nude arrived, so it was left on the lawn in front of her house. Her Sheridan

Circle neighbors, aghast at the stone sculpture, forbade their children to rollerskate near it. Then local wags kidnapped it, dragged it to the middle of the circle, and left it under the tail of General Sheridan's bronze horse.

The police were caught in the middle. They appreciated the sensibilities of the community; they were equally aware of the rights of the statue's owner. So they compromised by hauling the poor girl back to Mrs. Barney's lawn and raising a canvas tent over her to protect the public from her—and vice versa.

Smithson's Bones

It's typical of the Smithsonian to have its founder, born in 1765, on the premises—not just a likeness, though it has that, too, but his very bones. The skeleton of James Smithson—chemist, mineralogist, and illegitimate son of an English nobleman, who left his fortune to establish an institution in a country he never visited—lies entombed directly inside the entrance to the Castle (the original Smithsonian Building).

Smithson didn't leave his bones to anyone—but his offspring institution claimed them, and in 1904 sent Alexander Graham Bell to a cemetery in Genoa, Italy, to fetch them. At the exhumation in a pelting snowstorm, Mrs. Bell photographed the remains. And in Washington, President Theodore Roosevelt sent the Marine band to welcome the bones to their new home.

A second resettling of the bones took place during the refurbishing of the Castle crypt in 1973. It wasn't even known then if the bones were inside the urn, or in the block of marble, or in the floor. As it turned out, they were in a casket inside the block of marble.

The bones were removed, gingerly, from the casket, covered with a tablecloth, and carried across the Mall to a lab in the Museum of Natural History. There, curator Lawrence Angel, one of the Smithsonian's forensic anthropologists, studied his man. Such scrutiny is the greatest of pleasures to Angel, which is why he's been called the Sherlock of Bones (many are the remains of unidentified victims he's sleuthed for the FBI).

Smithson, Angel reported, stood five feet six inches tall. He had a chest that was "not small," strong arms, large hands, and "something funny" about his upper right arm— a different torsion angle. The result of an accident? Or of fencing, perhaps? The wear on one tooth suggests a pipe stem in frequent use. Though Smithson's health apparently was all right from later childhood on, he was malnourished in early childhood. Angel has no doubt about it. Tooth enamel shows the condition, and so does the pelvic structure and the low base of his skull.

Warming to his subject as the report progressed, Angel noted knee retroversion angles that are more tilted than usual, suggesting, he said, some adaptation to hill or mountain climbing. He summed up Smithson as vigorous and active, a man who climbed, worked with his hands, and spent much time bent over a desk. He also provided portrait sketches, based on tracings of the skull. They show a long face with a prominent aquiline nose, a strong chin, and a wide, low, sloping brow (our benefactor was lower browed, according to Angel, than according to Smithson's portraitist).

Three days after the bones were removed, they were returned to their monument, sealed in a copper box. The respectful examination of them—besides adding information to a skimpy record—seems to have laid to rest a rumored Castle ghost, which was manifesting itself as mysterious lights in the night, strange trips of an empty elevator, and books jumping from shelves. All's quiet now, nights, at the Castle.

Andy Jackson's Rejected Tomb

On the east terrace of the Museum of American History is an ancient stone sarcophagus. It is one of two that were picked up in Beirut by Commodore Jesse Elliott of the U.S. Navy, loaded aboard the frigate *Constitution*, the famous "Old Ironsides," and shipped back to the States in 1839 as ballast.

Ornamentation and an inscription on one of these portable tombs seemed to indicate that it had been slated to hold the remains of a Roman emperor. In a burst of enthusiasm for ex-President Andrew Jackson, who had returned to Tennessee after his second term, Commodore Elliott and some other officials suggested that he be placed in one of the sarcophagi when he went to address the great Congress on high.

Of course Jackson was horrified at the thought. An imperial resting place for an Old Indian fighter who had made political hay out of his simple democratic tastes? Never!

Since no one knew what else to do with them, the sarcophagi were given away. One went to Bryn Mawr, which may or may not have wanted it. The other was set up beside the Smithsonian Castle, then moved to the Museum of American History. It's still empty—as far as anyone knows.

—

The Great Brain Contest

Major John Wesley Powell, Civil War hero and explorer of the Grand Canyon, had one of the biggest brains in history. He doesn't have it any more. The Smithsonian does. It weighs almost a kilogram and a half and lies on a bed of cotton batting in a jar of alcohol, upstairs at the Museum of Natural History. Of course, there's a story behind all this.

Powell was a feisty, vigorous scientist who had lost an

arm at Shiloh. In 1869, while on a Smithsonian-sponsored survey of the Colorado River, he became the first white man to get through the length of the Grand Canyon by boat—an extraordinary achievement. Largely because of his explorations, Powell was made director of the relatively new U.S. Geographical and Geological Survey.

One of Powell's colleagues was W.J. (he always used just the initials) McGee, an ethnologist, fascinated with many arcane scientific theories and studies, including phrenology, which was very popular in the mid-19th century. He and Powell apparently got to talking about the size of their respective brains and ended up willing them to each other. Dr. Edward A. Spitzka, an eminent Philadelphia brain surgeon, was to decide which brain was bigger.

Powell died first, in 1902. It turned out that, brainy as he undoubtedly was, he had forgotten to tell his family about

the pact with McGee. It was a bit awkward, but a gentleman's agreement was not to be taken lightly, so McGee
ended up with Powell's brain, nicely pickled. He delivered
it to Dr. Spitzka, who was delighted with it. He had long
regretted that the only brains he got to study came from
"ne'er-do-well paupers and criminals."

Spitzka wrote a 60-page analysis of Powell's brain and
read his paper before the Anthropological Society of Washington. It was a beautiful brain, all right, just a tad smaller
than Thackeray's (apparently a record-breaker) and in the
ball park with Daniel Webster's, which was the admiration
of all brain fanciers. Spitzka explained how each lobe and
cranny accounted for Powell's mental achievements—his
interest in and sympathy for the Indians, his administrative
ability, and his imaginative concepts.

When McGee died some years later, he left his body to
a medical school and his brain to Dr. Spitzka for comparison
with Powell's. W.J.'s brain was a good effort, but lost to
Powell's by 78 grams.

■

Dummies and Doubles

The Smithsonian's Charlie McCarthy is the original wooden
Charlie, not the later-model Charlie made of fiber glass. He

came to the American History Museum after ventriloquist Edgar Bergen's death, along with puppets Mortimer Snerd and Effie Klinker—the trio known as "the kids," who had enjoyed a room to themselves in the Bergen home.

The Smithsonian's Howdy Doody, though, isn't strictly speaking the original Howdy of the 1950s television show. He's exactly like him, down to the last freckle and overalls button, but he was one of the two stand-ins, sometimes called Double Doody. All the same, he's so important to the collections that when a curator traveled back to the museum with him in her Pullman compartment (he didn't fit overhead and she was not about to trust him to a baggage car), she let him have—in his carrying case and duffle bag—three quarters of the bed.

—

Lindbergh and the "Spirit"

Back when the *Spirit of St. Louis* used to hang in the Arts and Industries Building, along with the Wright brothers' plane and a few other extraordinary relics, people would sometimes notice a tall gentleman up on the balcony, looking down on the *Spirit* with a strangely proprietary air. It was, as you've guessed, Charles Lindbergh himself. He exercised the utmost tact in checking on his old ocean-spanning aircraft, but check he did. He felt he owed that much to the wonderful old Ryan that got him to Paris in 1927.

Paul Garber, then curator of airplanes, would stand guard over these Lindbergh visits so that the General wouldn't be bothered by tourists while he came to commune with his plane.

One day Lindbergh informed Garber that he needed to get into the cabin of the *Spirit* to see if he could find some pencil marks he had scribbled during his historic flight. Would that be possible?

Of course, said Garber. Come in the evening, when the crowds have gone.

Lindbergh came, and the two wrestled a tall stepladder under the airplane. Garber held it while Lindbergh shinnied up and scrambled aboard. Then, as Garber tells the tale, Lindbergh disappeared inside and Garber sat alone on a bench beneath, thinking of other things in the lonely, half-darkened hall.

And while dreaming away in the silence, he suddenly heard a voice from above: "I'm all ready, now."

He looked up, and there was the *Spirit of St. Louis,* gently rocking at about the right altitude for flaring out to touch down at Le Bourget Field in Paris. And there was Lindbergh's head sticking out of the cabin window as it had when he judged his height on that momentous May night.

Garber says he shook his head as if to clear a vision. Only at the Smithsonian could that scene have occurred. And only at the Smithsonian could Lindbergh's purpose have been so amply fulfilled. For he had made those pencil marks during the flight to indicate the rate at which he was burning fuel from the various tanks. He needed the information for his new book, *The Spirit of St. Louis.*

And, of course, the marks were all there, just as Lindbergh had left them. People don't mess with the great treasures of the Institution.

—

A Thousand Scrapbooks

At the Cooper-Hewitt Museum in New York, people interested in design can find just about anything they want. If it's not immediately accessible, it's pretty sure to be among the two million items noted in more than 1,000 scrapbooks that are available for the asking.

The books were started by the Hewitt sisters, Miss Sarah and Miss Eleanor, who spent most of their lives collecting things like lamps and laces and wallpaper and drawings and porcelains. What they didn't collect, they filed in their well-indexed scrapbooks. They filled these books with illustrations ripped out of magazines and even expensive books to round out their records of such topics as Angels, French Beds, Bird Cages, Door Knobs, Drawer Pulls, and Knockers. And they added all the things they collected, as well.

The items and the knowledge all came together in 1897, when the Hewitt ''girls'' opened their museum of the decorative arts for the use of designers and scholars and mere students. It's been part of the Smithsonian since 1968, scrapbooks and all.

—

The Case of
the Bus Rider's Shoe

Hirshhorn Museum visitors are generally brought up short by a strange sculpture of four life-size figures done in plaster: George Segal's *Bus Riders*. Three are seated, one stands. And all have that lonely self-absorption so inevitable in a situation where strangers are grouped close together physically, yet remain apart.

It's a haunting piece of work, ghostly white, the rough plaster giving a blurred impression of clothes and facial features, as though the whole thing were eerily out of focus—yet so real that you wonder how in the world Segal did it.

For one thing, he picked up real bus seats from a dump. One is not taken, the rider preferring to stand behind it— and when you see it, you find it so familiar and prosaic that the figures around it become especially unworldly. Also, incidentally, that empty seat is a devilish temptation to tourists. The Hirshhorn guards are forever shooing away people who want to be photographed while sitting in it.

Segal got the figures from life—literally. He talked four friends into suffering through the claustrophobic business of being molded in plaster. Then he cracked the molds open and let his models out, resealing the figures afterward.

But a fourth-grade boy on a school trip pointed out to a guard that if you look carefully at one of the plaster feet, you'll see, through a nick, that there's a shoe inside. The guard couldn't explain that. He walked away uneasily. And the school group left with slightly troubled minds.

And everyone now wonders, way down deep: *Is there anything inside the shoe?*

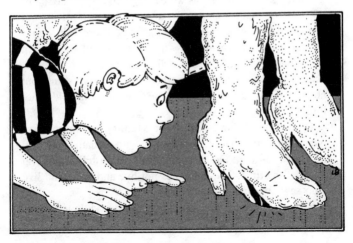

George Washington, Shirtless

In sculpting a 12-ton George Washington without a shirt, American artist Horatio Greenough let his artistic conscience be his guide. Where Congress had commissioned a colossal standing figure, Greenough seated his man, opting to clothe him in virtue—and a bit of classical drapery.

Greenough had chiseled away at his Carrara marble for eight years and must have felt gratified when his huge masterwork, on its way from his studio in Florence, Italy, to the seaport of Leghorn, in a cart pulled by 22 oxen, inspired local folk to kneel by the road. (They took bed-sheeted George for a saint.)

All the same, complaints were registered early. The sculptor was assessed for damage to roadside trees en route. And that, in 1841, was only the beginning. There followed a series of expensive moves—into the Capitol rotunda in Washington, D.C., and out again—a reject—onto the east Capital grounds, where temporary sheds through some, but not all, of 67 winters protected the General from cold if not insult.

In the end, Congress was out $42,000 and more for a memorial statue that offended many with its bath-time likeness of a reserved and formal subject. As a fellow general put it at the time: The man does not live and never did live who saw Washington without his shirt.

Since 1908, the Smithsonian has given asylum to Greenough's George Washington. In 1962, moved once more, the Founding Father was installed in the new National Museum of History and Technology (now American History), where visitors find him today a mildly ha ha figure—directing traffic to the escalators with upraised hand.

■

Charles Freer
and the Gift That Almost Wasn't

Charles Lang Freer made his pile in railroading. He started from scratch, worked hard, got some breaks, and finally emerged as the brain behind the formation of American Car and Foundry. By 1900, aged 46, he was rich enough to retire and devote himself to his passion for collecting art. With the advice and guidance of his friend James McNeill Whistler, Freer built a superb, meticulously discriminating collection of Oriental art.

In 1905 Charles Abbot, who would later become Secretary of the Smithsonian, noted that "a man named Freer from Detroit came through" and began negotiations for leaving his collection to the Institution—and so to the United States. It seems incredible to anyone who has visited the Freer Gallery on the Mall, but the fact is, no one seemed very eager to accept the gift. President Theodore Roosevelt set up a committee to look over Freer's items, and the report was at best lukewarm. No member of the committee knew or cared much about Oriental art, and Freer's manner put everyone off.

He was a fastidious man, careful about his celluloid collars and his Vandyke beard. He affected a walking stick. One of his friends described him as a man who "knows what he wants and gets it and then keeps still about it." Another summed him up neatly: "Charlie Freer is a killjoy at a picnic." When he showed off his treasures to the committee members, he made no special effort to educate them in Oriental art. Instead, he seated his guests on cushions and window seats and had his manservant bring out one jade disc after another, then blades and bowls and bronze vessels and all the rest, all shown at an unhurried pace, without much explanation.

The parade of beautiful pieces and paintings dragged on for four days and drove the committee up the wall. One member, Senator John Henderson of Missouri, summed up the feelings of all when he said that the things were all very well of their kind, "but damn the kind!"

It took President Roosevelt's clout to persuade the Smithsonian. For a naturalist-big-game-hunter-writer-politician, he knew a good deal about art, and he recognized the merit of Freer's collections. He laid on a White House dinner honoring the Smithsonian Regents and jollied things along until, still somewhat reluctant, they agreed to accept Freer's offer.

———

Arabella and Anita in Orbit

You have to have some drag with a curator at the Air and Space Museum to see Arabella and Anita, but their story is a good one. They were highly important to the United States space program.

In 1973 a school girl devised a project for Skylab II: Find out what kind of a web a weightless spider spins. NASA was delighted and designed cages, lights, and cameras triggered by sensors. Then the agency recruited a couple of common cross spiders, *Araneus diadematus*. They seemed to be the right stuff—unflappable, yet copious producers (especially the females) of orb-shaped webs, so regular in pattern that deviations are easy to spot. The astrospiders who made it into space were Arabella and her back-up, Anita.

On the first day in orbit, Arabella simply couldn't seem to get down to business. Working in fits and starts, she spun sloppy webs. Obviously, she was feeling the effects of weightlessness and possibly staring out at the view. By Day Three she was back in form, doing her stuff just as though she were back in the old cabbage patch. The webs were finer in space. That was pretty much expected. But the pattern remained the same.

The photographs of the webs, both aloft and aground, are in a curatorial office. Magnified 400 times, the webs plainly reveal their differences. And nearby are Arabella and Anita themselves, wispy little tangles floating in alcohol, memorialized by the Smithsonian for their small, vital part in increasing knowledge.

—

"No Tents Allowed— Not Even George Washington's!"

George Washington's headquarters tent takes up a remarkable amount of room in the military section of the Museum of American History. It deserves to, for it's a valuable relic of the old soldier. But it once caused adverse comment.

In 1896 the tent was set up on the Mall so photographs could be taken of it. And it happened that Col. John Wilson drove by in his carriage and saw the tent. Colonel Wilson was in charge of public grounds and buildings, and kept a sharp eye on the Mall to make sure it remained a clean, untrammeled parkland.

According to the *Washington Star*, Wilson stared at the old headquarters tent, then leapt from his carriage and delivered a salvo about as powerful as the British cannonballs that had occasionally hummed past the white canopy in earlier days. Who had the audacity, he demanded, to put up a lemonade booth on the national preserve?

—

The Story behind
a Giant Landscape

Albert Bierstadt's wall-size painting, *The Sierra Nevada in California*, strikes the eyes of visitors to the National Museum of American Art with a physical jolt. It is a huge, smashing celebration of the grandness of the West, as seen by the easterners who first marveled at those mountains— such a far cry from the soft Appalachian hills, painted by the Hudson River School.

Bierstadt, born in Germany, felt the full impact of the western scene during travels that stretched off and on for ten years. He didn't paint on the spot, however. This canvas was done in Rome in 1868 and bought two years later by William Dinsmore for his Hudson River mansion.

In 1977 the great painting, worth $1,200,000, was given to the Smithsonian by Dinsmore's great-granddaughter. The only catch was that it had been removed from its frame and stuck to a curved wall at the head of a flight of stairs. Smithsonian conservators would somehow have to pry it off—60 square feet of immensely valuable canvas held in place on the wall by brittle glue.

They went at it carefully with spatulas, chipping at the glue, gradually peeling the painting from the plaster. At last they freed it and sandwiched it between boards for transportation back to Washington. They were just lugging it out to the truck when a maid appeared and asked if they didn't want the frame, too—the one out in the barn.

Of course they did. They got another truck for it and then spent hours peeling off the bird droppings that covered the gold leaf.

■

Whistler's Father—
and Mother (by FDR)

The Freer Gallery's collection of James McNeill Whistler paintings includes a portrait of his father—not very good. His famous portrait of his mother is at the Louvre. But the Smithsonian *does* have a Whistler's Mother, of sorts, over at the Museum of American History.

It's a pencil sketch of the Whistler portrait, executed by Franklin D. Roosevelt, President of the United States. It's not bad, either.

The story behind it is that FDR, a long-time stamp collector, sometimes sent suggestions for new stamps to his Postmaster General, James Farley. The President, a talented man, would sketch his ideas. In 1934 Roosevelt suggested—and Farley accepted—a Mothers' Day stamp featuring Whistler's Mother. Denomination: three cents.

—

"That Can't Be Me!"

People who sat for portraits in the early days of daguerreotypes and photographs were generally astonished at the mirror quality of the results. They saw their own faces with a previously unknown clarity—and often they didn't much like the image. John Quincy Adams was the first President to pose. "All hideous," he said of his own features when he saw the daguerreotype now at the National Portrait Gallery.

Abraham Lincoln, the first President to be photographed extensively while in office, posed 120 times in all, and the Smithsonian has 25 photographs of him. Lincoln's last sitting, three days before his assassination, produced the famous cracked-plate photograph by Alexander Gardner that hangs in the National Portrait Gallery's Meserve Collection. Lincoln probably never saw the one print that Gardner made. But generally, when shown his own likeness, he would call it "true," and then add something like, "but not pretty."

Henry David Thoreau posed only once for a daguerreotype, and the Portrait Gallery has the result. A fan from

Michigan requested it, and sent Thoreau five dollars to cover the cost, so in his own words: "While in Worcester this week, I obtained the accompanying daguerreotype—which my friends think is pretty good—though better looking than I." Of course, Thoreau's friends were not exactly kind about the writer's looks. One said his face was like "some retired philosophic woodchuck or magnanimous fox."

Ernest Hemingway generally liked raffish pictures of himself. His friend Man Ray recalled taking one such in the Paris of 1923 during "a little party at my place." Hemingway had tried to pull the toilet chain and instead pulled a skylight down on himself.

"I put a small felt hat jauntily on his head," Man Ray recalled, "partly hiding the bandage—the wound wasn't serious—and took a picture." It's at the National Portrait Gallery, and of all Hemingway portraits, there is perhaps, as Man Ray said, "none which gave him the same look of amusement and indifference to the ups and downs of his career."

■

Vials of Earbones Come in Handy

Most people wouldn't know an otolith if they met one. But to a marine zoologist, otoliths, or earbones, are as plentiful and meaningful as the words in a textbook. In fish, they may be the size of a fingernail, maybe almost microscopic. And they have two attributes that make them important to science: They dissolve much more slowly than other fish bones; they are different for every fish species.

So, at the Museum of Natural History, otoliths in little vials fill many a shelf in the upstairs areas that visitors seldom see. They have been collected from the stomachs of whales and provide a sure tally of the species of fish a whale has eaten recently.

If Smithsonian sightseers should come face to face with a lineup of otoliths, they'd hurry past without a twitch of interest. But to a whale expert, such an array would be a dietary record, vastly useful in the struggle to preserve the gentle giants at the sea, whose own otoliths are apt to be the size of a grapefruit.

Gift Whiskers—
in Red, White, and Blue

A citizen of Downey, California, saluted the Nation's Bicentennial by growing a beard, which he shaved off, dyed red, white, and blue, and packed off to the Smithsonian.

Not everyone's whiskers are welcome, to be sure, but the young woman at American History who received this startling gift in the mail, instantly saw a place for it—in a temporary exhibit called *The Nation's Attic*. There—along with other oddball items such as flag snippets, whiskey-barrel-ends, and the sky-blue toothbrush shared by astronauts Borman and Lovell during their journey around the moon, not to mention historic gallstones and tobacco plugs and curbside bricks incised "Don't Spit!"—she paired up the colorful new beard with an old fake gray mustache found at the scene of an attempted mail-train robbery near Salt Lake City (and saved by postal authorities as evidence).

Patriotic-looking as the beard was, she kept it a respectful distance from the 19th-century framed collection of hair of the presidents and "other Persons of Distinction."

—

Sweet-Talking Curtiss Out of Two Airplanes

In the 1920s Mitchell Field, Long Island, was one of the world's great airports. In 1925 air races were held there, and Glenn Curtiss, the famous plane designer, showed up with a slick little racer that won the Pulitzer trophy for speed.

One of the onlookers was young Paul Garber of the Smithsonian. He was the museum's airplane man, short in stature and long in determination—and charm.

Garber knew all about Curtiss, every chapter in the designer's history from the time he was the fastest bicycling messenger boy in Rochester, New York. And when, after the races, Curtiss trotted out his first famous plane, the *Headless Pusher* of 1912, and sat at the controls for the sake of a few photographs, Garber went to work on him.

What about donating that marvelous, historic, important plane to the Smithsonian Institution?

Curtiss sat in the open seat, his hands on the wheel that controlled the flight surfaces. He turned toward one of his associates and said, "If I give away this airplane after all the money spent to restore it, I'll be fired by my own company!"

Then he turned back to Garber and said, okay, it's a deal. He even promised to find a 1912 engine and 1912 controls.

Garber then noted that the new prize-winning Curtiss Racer would also look good in the Smithsonian, and Glenn Curtiss went for that, too. So both planes now grace the National Air and Space Museum: the *Headless Pusher*, beautiful and historic; the racer in army colors, wearing the floats with which it won the Schneider Cup with Jimmy Doolittle at the controls.

■

When Mamie Broke
the Rules

If you give something to the Smithsonian, you can't borrow it back. After the Archie Bunker chairs were donated to the Museum of American History, the producer of the TV show, "All in the Family," tried to borrow them back for a new series. The Smithsonian turned him down, and the show had to spend $5,000 to make copies of the originals (which came from Goodwill).

But once—just once—the Institution bent the rule. After Mamie Eisenhower donated her inauguration gown to the First Ladies display, she found herself facing a state occasion without a comfortable pair of shoes to wear. Why? Because the pink slippers that felt so good on her feet had gone to the Smithsonian along with that gown.

Mamie begged the Smithsonian to relax the rule just that once, and the Smithsonian relented. A White House limousine whispered up to the museum, and the chauffeur went inside. The pink slippers were quietly slipped off the Mamie Eisenhower mannequin and whisked back to the White House.

They were returned just as soon as the function was over, and they've never been removed again. But they did have one night on borrowed time.

—

Everything You'll Ever Need to Know about Wallpaper

The Smithsonian's Cooper-Hewitt Museum in New York has scraps, samples, and panels of some 7,000 wallpaper patterns—the world's most comprehensive collection. They range from late-18th-century French and English to today's machine-printed papers, including an Andy Warhol pop-art design of a checkerboard of . . . no, not Marilyn Monroe this time, but a close-up of a cow.

There are collarband boxes covered in wallpaper of the 1820s and a paper-lined fiddle case. And there is a patch of wallpaper, 13 layers deep, which was lifted from a house in Fairfield, Connecticut, and comprises a small history of wallpaper tastes, from early-19th-century rainbow pattern to modern maroon grapes.

Of course, restorers and preservationists make use of the Cooper-Hewitt's expertise. When Mark Twain's fine old Victorian home in Hartford, Connecticut, was being renewed, the museum supplied the pattern for the dining room. Then one of the restorers showed up at the Cooper-Hewitt with a scrap of paper from behind the nursery mantelpiece. Did the museum know anything about this?

The Cooper-Hewitt expert studied the little piece and identified it: *Ye Frog He Would Awooing Go,* painted by Walter Crane in 1877. The museum didn't have it, but was able to steer the searcher to Utica, New York; to go to the bathroom of the Visiting Nurses Association; to look behind the wainscoting. . . . And there was the complete design available for copying.

—

Langley's Buzzards

One buzzard, one frigate bird, one bald eagle—a trio of large stuffed soaring birds—are the relics, almost 100 years later, of Samuel P. Langley's experiments with flight. The birds are scruffy now of feather and leaking tow, or it may be excelsior—their tattered look having to do with service in wind-tunnel experiments. Langley flew the birds in a circle at speeds of up to 60 miles an hour from a great steam-driven whirling arm he devised himself.

Astrophysicist Langley, the Smithsonian's third Secretary, fervently held to a notion that mechanical flight was possible. As a child lying in a New England pasture he'd watched a hawk flying overhead. For the longest time it sailed without a flap of its wings "as though it needed no work to sustain it, but was kept up there by some miracle."

In later years, Langley still watched—now the common turkey buzzard from the Aqueduct Bridge in Washington, D.C. It puzzled him that his fellow physicists never put their wits to it, never cared, as he cared, to understand "the way of a bird in the air."

At the National Zoo, Langley had a pair of towers built, 50 feet high, with canvas shelters on top. When visitors inquired, guards just shook their heads. But a newspaperman noticed that "once in a while, when a buzzard flies overhead, two men suddenly appear, one on top of each tower, and snap guns at the bird, thereupon retiring . . . from view." The weapons were cameras with gunstocks and triggers, and the marksmen were taking synchronized photographs of the birds in flight.

All of Langley's bird observations, his bird-wing drawings, and columns of computations recorded on the flimsy pages of his "wastebooks" (13 volumes of them, now at the Air and Space Museum), were preparations for building flying machines. Over the years, the Secretary tinkered continuously in the sheds behind the Smithsonian Castle and tested little models on the Mall. Passersby were delighted, his colleagues were embarrassed—one of them remarking that a trip to heaven would be flight enough for *him*. In all, Langley tested more than 100 models, the first powered by twisted rubber bands. Then he built structures capable of carrying engines. He called these his aerodromes.

Langley knew his major problem was balance and guidance. The slightest breeze had currents and counter-currents going in all directions—to which buzzards adapted by rocking and balancing. How could artificial flight be as responsive? (The Wright brothers' solution—ailerons—eluded him.)

After thousands of experiments that didn't pan out, Aerodrome #5 finally took off from the roof of a houseboat on the Potomac River and "swept continuously through the air like a living thing," according to its maker. And when the fuel ran out, it landed gently on the water, having covered more than half a mile. The date was May 6, 1896.

Aerodrome #5 looked something like a dragonfly—with tandem sets of wings, 13 feet tip to tip. It weighed 30 pounds. The War Department pressed Langley to build a full-scale machine capable of carrying a man. The Secretary agreed, and for five years, work went forward in great secrecy in the Castle-yard sheds. In public Langley kept a scholarly reserve, but others expressed wild expectations. According to a *Chicago Times* account, his flying machine would be able to dart down upon a sinking ship and snatch its passengers from peril.

Finally, the new aerodromic bird, dubbed the *Buzzard*, was ready. Launch was set for July 1903. Reporters gathered—and waited. What with little failures of one sort and another, they still waited three months later.

Then on October 2, at noon, with the weather and things mechanical being just about right, Charles Manley, Langley's gifted mechanic, took his seat between the engine and the front bearing, his head just inches from the propellers. Amid skyrocket bursts and blasts from tugs, Manley waved; the reporters in their little boats waved back. The great aerodrome was flung into the sky 50 feet above the water line—only to dive nose-first into the river. All that was seen was widening circles on the surface until Manley emerged, swimming.

"BUZZARD A WRECK/LANGLEY'S HOPES DASHED," the *Washington Post* announced.

The fault, it seemed, lay in the launching device, which caught the rear end of the plane. At a second launch, it functioned no better. By this time, in December, ice had formed on the river, and Manley was painfully injured.

Langley felt there had never been a proper flight test, but by now the press jeered. Congressmen were cruelly humorous, citing expenditures of $50,000 for a mud duck. Let the Secretary stick to his stuffed birds and extinct Pterodactyls, said one. Tell Langley, the only thing he made fly was the government's money!

As it happened, just nine days after the Secretary's humiliating failure, Orville and Wilbur Wright flew their Flyer from the sands of Kitty Hawk, North Carolina. Langley's dream was fulfilled—though the glory was not his or his *Buzzard*'s.

Anna Cooper, Almost Forgotten

"People think history is what happens to the other fellow, not to their relatives," says Louise Hutchinson, staff historian at the Anacostia Neighborhood Museum. She came to this conclusion while putting together a museum show on the black educator, Anna Cooper, who died in Washington, aged 105, in 1964.

Searching for details about Anna, Hutchinson tried to visit the teacher's great-niece, who still lived in Anna's house. Hutchinson knew that Anna was the second black woman graduate of Oberlin and that her own high school students were the only blacks admitted to Ivy League universities without tutoring. But not until the great-niece, after 18 months of negotiation, allowed her to rummage around in the Cooper house, did Hutchinson find some much-sought personal history.

Behind a radiator was Anna's Oberlin diploma. Her doctorate certificate from the Sorbonne was out in the gazebo. And serving as a bookmark in a heavily scribbled copy of the *Aeneid* was a dingy postcard written by Anna—then 25 and teaching at Wilberforce University—to her mother.

To Hutchinson, the affection and esteem expressed in that postcard fitted what was known of Anna Cooper's childhood. Anna's father had been white, a member of one of America's oldest families, and Anna felt she owed him "not a sou." But her mother had been a slave, struggling into freedom, and Anna's happiest childhood memories were of teaching her mother to read.

For the historian, it all now came together. "It takes time," says Louise Hutchinson, "to understand that clutter and family trash may be valuable."

—

The 100-Year-Old Solar Scientist

Charles Greeley Abbot, the Smithsonian's fifth Secretary, was a New Hampshire farm boy who intended to become a carpenter. He became a physicist instead, and was hired by the Institution in 1895 to work in the astrophysical lab. His field was the sun. He observed, measured, computed, and recorded solar radiation, its energy and its effects on weather.

More than three-quarters of a century later he was still at it, at age 100, working in an office in the northwest tower of the Castle. In that lifetime Abbot invented and improved upon some 20 complex instruments for measuring the sun's energy. He established that solar radiation fluctuates in cycles and that it's related to the weather. He also found time to serve as Secretary from 1928 to 1944.

After Dr. Abbot died (at 101), an empty box of Quick Mother's Oats showed up among his lab relics. Around the jumbo-size container was wrapped a 16-foot sheet of paper crowded with columns of figures—figures for every month for the 63 years from 1896 to 1959. They were some of Dr. Abbot's observations of the weather as related to radiation fluctuations. People recalled that he was always glad to suggest dates for upcoming weddings—when his records indicated that there would be no rain.

Abbot also cooked small gingerbread cakes in his solar oven—heated by mirrors that gradually rotated to focus the sun's rays—and served them to his staff. Then he'd sing sea chanteys and dance with the secretaries.

—

George Washington's Teeth

Lots of people think they know about George Washington's false teeth, but few really do. Except, of course, at the Smithsonian, where one of the President's last sets has been on display. It dates from 1795 and is a splendidly complex arrangement of gold and hippopotamus ivory, the work of John Greenwood, the finest dentist in the young United States.

Greenwood was the son of a craftsman who had advertised

himself as a maker of umbrellas, artificial legs, and false teeth. The youngster probably watched teeth in the making. Anyway, after serving in the Revolution, John declared himself a dentist and circulated handbills in New York which declared that Greenwood teeth "give a youthful air to the countenance" and "render pronunciation more agreeable and distinct."

Washington met Greenwood in 1789, the year that he became President. He had been continually bothered by his teeth since his youth. From all accounts they looked all right, but they ached and abscessed despite all the washes and potions and "spunge" toothbrushes that he used on them. The first one was yanked out when he was only 22, and from then on he lost about one a year. By the time Greenwood got into the act, Washington had only one natural tooth left in his head—a lower left premolar.

Greenwood took over, and sets of teeth went back and forth between the President and the dentist, who soon was wearing that final Washington tooth on his watch chain. Much correspondence also flowed between the two, including a letter from Greenwood filled with the sort of advice that dentists love to hand out. The last dentures the President had sent him, wrote Greenwood (who was not strong on spelling and punctuation), were "very black," their color "Ocationed either by your soaking them in port wine, or by your drinking it. Port wine being sower, takes of [sic] all the polish. . . . I advice you to Either, take them out. After dinner and put them in cleain water, and put in another sett, or Cleain them with a brush and some Chalk scraped

fine, it will absorbe the Acid which Collects from the mouth, and preserve them longer. . . ." Possibly because hippo ivory is startlingly white, the dentist added, "If you want your teeth more yellower soake them in Broath or pot liquer, but not in tea or Acid."

There remain several sets of Washington teeth (none of them made of wood) and some partial plates. A great-great-grandaughter of Lord Cornwallis living in Latin America has half a broken lower plate. Washington lost it at Trenton, when he mounted up in haste after the battle there. British soldiers found it in a barn and gave it to their commander, the same man who five years later surrendered to Washington at Yorktown. You'd think Cornwallis might have returned them, but apparently he knew a souvenir when he saw one.

Civil War Kilroys

The little wooden post office of Headsville, West Virginia, stands beside the Constitution Avenue entrance of the Museum of American History. It was moved there board by board and set up exactly as it had stood in its small home town. On its shutters are the same old advertisements—for Foutz's liniment and Handsford's Balsam of Myrrh.

But on the backs of those wooden shutters are the graffiti of both Union and Confederate soldiers who passed through Headsville during the Civil War. The spelling is often pretty far-fetched, the full sense generally lost, but the big message that comes through is that soldiers have always and will always scribble their ''Kilroy was here'' when they have a chance.

On April 18, 1863 (less than three months before Gettysburg), the 14th Regiment (Virginia) halted here, and it seems that just about all of Company D signed one shutter. William Winans, in fact, wrote his name at least three times. Elsewhere an ''ofiser,'' quite possibly Yankee, is described as ''one hell of a fool'' and a ''squirt.'' And four lines of verse indicate that there was at least one young Federal with a touch of unblushing patriotism:

A union of Lakes and a Union of Lands
A union of States none can Sever
A union of hearts and a Union of hands
But the flag of our union forever.

■

How the Ashanti Measured Gold

Hundreds of little brass figures can be seen at the National Museum of African Art. They take the form of fish, insects, tiny crocodiles, little knives, and humans going about their everyday activities. There is a small sculpture of two old men shaking hands; another of a man sacrificing a chicken.

The little items were used to measure gold dust when it was the medium of currency in Ghana, back when that country was called the Gold Coast. The weights were made by the lost-wax method of metal casting. An artisan would fashion a wax figure, then pack clay around it. When the clay was fired, the wax melted and only the mold of the figure was left in the fired clay. Then liquid bronze could be poured into the mold. It became an accurate—and entertaining—weight, typifying the African knack of turning a prosaic item into a pleasing and amusing design.

—

Why the Tri-motor Had
a Hole in Its Roof

If you visit the Hall of Air Transportation at the National Air and Space Museum in the evening, you can learn something about the great old Ford Tri-motor, hanging from the ceiling, that you otherwise would never notice: It once had a hole in its roof. When the night lights are on, and the sky is dark, you can see, reflected in one of the transparent ceiling bubbles above the plane, the reflection of a round patch in the roof of the old corrugated aluminum fuselage. The story of the patch is part of that plane's history.

Henry Ford was an ardent pacifist who once called airplanes "damned warmaking machines." That didn't stop him, however, from manufacturing Liberty engines during World War I. And when William Stout, a top-notch aircraft designer, asked Ford for $1,000—"and I can only promise you one thing. You'll never see it again"—Ford cracked open his checkbook and so got into the airplane manufacturing business.

Ford made a tremendous investment in aviation, and the Tri-motor was a hit with the public, which, thanks to Lindbergh's historic flight, had become air-happy. But the plane wasn't exactly comfortable. Passengers sat in single wicker seats separated by an aisle and put up with tooth-rattling vibration, ear-shattering noise, and so much ponderous bucking around at the low levels of the flights that it was difficult for many to keep down the box lunches that the copilot served. The lavatory was a chilling experience, for it offered only the simplest facility imaginable—a hole that opened in the bottom of the aircraft. The copilot had to somehow make his way back to the tail section to perform another of his tasks—sorting the mail.

Nevertheless, old-timers look upon the Smithsonian's Tri-motor with nostalgia, though many wonder about the bottom of the fuselage, which is smooth instead of corrugated. The fact is, the museum's Ford was a 43-year-old workhorse with 50,000 flying hours when it was acquired. It had flown New York-Boston-Montreal, also Cleveland-Los Angeles and Los Angeles-Chicago. It changed hands a score of times, did service in Nicaragua and Honduras, dusted crops in Montana, flew cargo in Alaska. It was modified many times. Finally, when a pilot overshot his landing at Oaxaca, Mexico, the plane wound up in a weedy dump, 500 yards off the end of the gravel strip. And a family of five moved into it.

This explains the hole in the roof. It was cut for the chimney of a pot-bellied stove. Patching it was one of the myriad items of restoration that museum experts put the old veteran through after they got hold of it.

There's lots more to do to make the Tri-motor an accurate, early 1930s transport. The instrumentation is wrong. So are the seats, which ought to be the fondly remembered wicker. Propellers are constant-speed instead of ground-adjustable. Engines don't have the right horsepower. Wheels and tires aren't the original type.

But the huge, bulky, awkward old "Flying Washboard" remains a great favorite of curators as well as visitors. And at least nobody's living in it anymore.

Komodo Dragons

A former National Zoo director, Ted Reed, was given the job of escorting some birds to Indonesia as a present from Attorney General Robert Kennedy to President Sukarno. In gratitude for Reed's concerned care, the Indonesian president unexpectedly offered him a pair of Komodo dragons as ''a gift for the children of the United States.''

Komodo dragons are spectacular giant lizards, and Reed was delighted to accept these two for the zoo. They were put into cages in the United States compound to await shipment to Washington. And then, apparently unimpressed by getting a free trip to the States, the male escaped inside the compound.

How do you handle a nine-foot Komodo dragon? The American staff wrung their hands helplessly; the U.S. Marine guards fingered their rifles. But Ted Reed asked for a broom and gently swept the huge creature back into its shipping cage.

Ella, Amazing Grace, and the Pomo Baskets

Among the millions of articles that have been sent to the Natural History Museum are a collection of Pomo Indian baskets from California. They were amassed by a wealthy but lonely woman named Ella Hubby, who had bought many of them from a woman dealer, "Amazing Grace" Nicholson. At the turn of the century, Amazing Grace used to travel to the Klamath River Indian communities by canoe and—in Gibson Girl blouse and long skirt—spend days joining the Pomo women in their chores. In return, she learned how they made their baskets, and why.

All were finely woven with a willow warp and a pattern of gold sedges used as thread to contrast with the dark brown bullrush fibers. Many baskets were for food, but the nicest were for ceremonial use and were adorned with bits of clam and abalone shell and mallard and meadowlark feathers. Some of these were as small as a cup. They probably would have been presents for births or marriages and then would have been burned on funeral pyres.

Ella Hubby paid Amazing Grace as much as $500 for a good basket—a lot of money around 1900—and by 1920, having carried scores of them with her as she traveled back and forth to the east, Ella was ready to turn them over to the Smithsonian. She offered them, saying they were examples of "a dying art among a dying people." The Smithsonian agreed. It now has 400 of the California baskets, a monument to Ella and Amazing Grace.

—

Happy Birthday to the Renwick

Fourteen birthday cakes were the winners of a contest celebrating the tenth anniversary of the Smithsonian's crafts museum, the Renwick. And the prizewinning cakes stayed on as part of the permanent collection. One cake was made of glowing neon, one of glass, one of crocheted yarn. Others were fashioned of stuffed fabric, of porcelain, of earthenware, and of steel.

A second contest welcomed sample souvenirs—all featuring the ornate red-sandstone Renwick building. Artists submitted postcards made of porcelain, also a gigantic puzzle-keychain crafted in a size to fill a tour bus, and a quilted tea cozy replica of the building itself, complete with the statues-in-niches and resident pigeons.

—

First Ladies' Secret

Carpeting wears out faster in the First Ladies Hall than at any other place in the Smithsonian museums. People flock there partly to see the gowns, partly to feel the tug of history. For the mannequins represent more than two-score stately figures, posed in groups as though affably chatting, in settings that carefully represent presidential rooms at various periods.

All are in the White House except for the first group: Martha Washington, who lived in Philadelphia (the White House hadn't been built), and, keeping her company in that setting, Abigail Adams and Martha Jefferson Randolph, who *did* live in the White House. The other First Ladies occupy six reproductions of White House rooms. The Blue Room appears twice—as it was in the late 19th century and again in 1900.

All the figures pose naturally with the gestures and mannerisms you would expect in a receiving line or some other painfully formal White House function. Hair-dos meticulously copy what is known from portraits and recollections. Heights vary from tiny Sarah Jackson (she was a mere five feet) to the lofty stature of some of the modern women (Eleanor Roosevelt appears to be the tallest). Eyes sometimes sparkle with interest, sometimes are modestly downcast. Expressions seem to vary with the personalities of the different First Ladies.

And yet. . . . Abruptly, you are aware of something that has, literally, been staring you in the face: The features of the First Ladies are all practically the same. They're based on a bust of Cordelia, King Lear's youngest daughter, sculpted in 1863 by Pierce F. Connelly of Louisiana. A copy of the original stands discreetly at the edge of the exhibit, just as a movie stand-in is tactfully segregated from the star. A dab of make-up here, a tease of curls there, and despite the same classical nose, rounded cheeks, and firm chin, each mannequin takes on her assigned character.

You might think that once you realize the First Ladies' secret, the impact of the exhibit would be spoiled. After all, how credible is a display in which Eleanor Roosevelt and Florence Harding are dead ringers for Jackie Kennedy? But the mannequins get away with it. People keep coming— among them some who send sharp notes when Grace Coolidge's sorority pin is a tad off-angle (though no one noticed when for years her flapper-style dress was on backward). And the carpet continues to wear out.

—

The Archeologist's Socks

It's something to bear in mind when you read impressive
figures like 70 million specimens in the Natural History
collections alone. Bering Sea Culture archeologist-emeritus
Henry Collins, Jr., once found that museum catalog numbers
had been affixed to his own footwear. On an Alaskan trip,
in the 1930s, he'd worn straw socks inside his boots, Eskimo-
style, to keep his feet dry. and he'd shipped them back along
with his collected objects, such as harpoon points and carvings. The unpackers were impressed—and logged in the
socks.

—

The Trouble with Blue Jeans

Visitors to the Museum of American History have long been
greeted by the giant Star-Spangled Banner that once flew
over Fort McHenry and inspired Francis Scott Key to write
the song that has become our national anthem. But now the
great flag is only on display for a few moments each hour.
The reason: the danger of dust.

When the old flag reappeared, a century after its night of
glory, a skilled seamstress, Amelia Fowler, enlisted a dozen
young needlewomen to rescue it by stitching the fragile

fabric to an Irish linen backing. They did a splendid job to save the banner that had survived English rockets and bombs in 1814 (ironically, Amelia Fowler was an Englishwoman), using open buttonhole stitches that formed a network of little rectangles across the flag's surface.

But over the years, dust caught in those rectangles, just as snow banks up on windowpanes. And the abrasive effect of the dust—which unfortunately doesn't melt the way snow does—began to eat at the ancient fabric. The conservation people analyzed the dust and found minerals from the soil of the Mall and various fibers, among them goodly amounts of microscopic bits of blue cotton.

Where from? Blue jeans, of course. Thousands of visitors had been wearing blue jeans in front of that flag for a couple of generations. And every time any one of the endless horde took a step, with that nice whisk of one pantleg against the other, the dust flew. And some of it—enough of it—eventually came to rest on the flag stitches.

One good thing about it: The flag's colors are well preserved, considering its age. All that dust helped shield the fabric from the fading effect of light.

▬

What's a *Hochochet*?

Word lists and grammars—Eskimo expressions for the weather, coastal Indians' seaweed vocabulary—have long been a preoccupation of Smithsonian collectors.

A 1970s dictionary of the Tzotzil Indians, Mayan corn farmers from southern Mexico, contains such a choice word as *hochochet*, which is defined as: ''scraping (sound of gobbler wings on ground when displaying, of branches dragged on ground or of drunk dragged by the arms).'' On the other hand, when pronounced explosively, as *hoch'och'et*, it means: ''rustling, scratching, shattering (glass), scraping (object on smooth surface), crashing, dragging logs.''

Anthropologist Robert Laughlin, who does this collecting with the aid of sound-effects records, says it's a specialty of Mayan languages to focus on sounds or shapes in motion.

He adds that he's heard a *hochochet* or two himself, as well as *ve'von*, which means: "woman walking, with wild hair, or flies swarming."

—

The Speed-Demon President

In the Museum of American History's transportation hall is a handsome black carriage with yellow wheels and wickerwork and brass lanterns. It's open, with seats unusually high to make room for compartments under them. All in all it was a perfect vehicle for an inaugural parade back in the innocent days when a President sat right out in the fresh air where everyone could see him.

It belonged to President Grant. He bought it in 1870, made to his order for $1,200, and he rode in it at his second inaugural. Wags said those compartments were for his bottles. Actually, they were specially built for hunting dogs—hence the open wickerwork. But Grant hated hunting and never owned a dog, so no one quite knows why he had them.

Grant's Inauguration Day, everyone agreed, was the coldest ever. Marching bands had to cope with frozen trumpet valves, and the Arctic air whipped tears from the eyes of drummer boys and turned them to ice on their cheeks. Yet all along Pennsylvania Avenue, Grant sat stoically in that open phaeton, taking the worst the weather could offer.

Grant always loved horses. He learned to drive at eight, to plow at eleven, and was rated the finest horseman of his West Point class. He liked to break away from the White House at 3 in the afternoon and visit the stables to check up on his racer, Butcher's Boy; his matched carriage horses, St. Louis and Egypt; his sons' Shetlands, Billy Button and Reb; and his own beloved Cincinnati, the dark bay charger that had carried him through the last 15 months of the Civil War. Cincinnati stood 17 hands tall, strode through city traffic as if it wasn't there, and would wait at a curb, unattended. One of the few people that Grant ever allowed to ride him was Abraham Lincoln.

The President liked to take his family for carriage rides in that sleek phaeton that stands in the Smithsonian, but what he liked to do most was to go *fast*. He liked to go so fast that his wife, Julia, often asked to be set down at the White House—now! One time Grant went dashing, solo, through Washington's streets, full tilt (some accounts say M Street, some say Boundary), when a police officer grabbed a bridle and brought the rig to a halt by letting himself be dragged along the street. He was a black policeman named William West, and when he saw whom he'd nabbed he was mortified.

Grant told him he was doing the right thing, and to get on with it. So officer West fined him and impounded the rig. The President climbed down from his seat and walked back to the White House.

He was the only President to be arrested for speeding while in office.

Painting the Ride
That Never Happened

The largest portrait at the National Portrait Gallery shows
"Grant and His Generals" in a 16-by-10-foot painting. The
27 men are supposedly riding toward Richmond, for Ole
Balling, the artist, joined Grant's headquarters during the
midst of that campaign. But such a ride never happened.
The generals were all over the country, not all together in
one place.

Balling went to Shenandoah to paint General Sheridan—
on Rienzi, the black horse whose name was changed to
Winchester after the battle in which he carried his master
20 miles to save the day. Winchester, stuffed, now graces
the military gallery at the Museum of American History.
As for General Sherman, Balling never caught up with him
until after the war. Then, when the artist asked him for a
sitting, William Tecumseh told him to "go to a hot place."

In the big group portrait, Grant is depicted wearing boots
that reach well above his knees. These are authentic. A New
York bootmaker made them without having seen the short-
statured General. They were a joke at Grant's headquarters.

—

The Million-Dollar Parcel

In 1958 New York jeweler Harry Winston offered the world's best-known gem, the Hope Diamond, to the Smithsonian. The news made headlines. But no one knew how Winston planned to deliver the goods.

He sent the 45.5-carat dark blue diamond through the U.S. Mail in a plain brown wrapper, stamped "Fragile" and "Registered Mail." The total charge came to $145.29, out of which $2.44 went for postage and the rest to pay for indemnities on a million-dollar parcel. Postal Service people now say the total didn't quite add up right, but allowing for clerical nervousness, it was close enough.

Harry Winston misaddressed the package. He sent it to the Smithsonian "Institute." The Institution got it all right, however, and overlooked the error.

The Jokes Artists Play

Only a few paintings at the Hirshhorn have glass covering them, or are fenced off to keep viewers beyond arm's length. One is a work by Martial Raysse called *Made in Japan*. It's a take-off on the famous *Odalisque*, painted in 1814 by Ingres, which hangs in the Louvre—a harem slave girl reclining on a couch amid Oriental silks. Here is the same girl, the same couch, but the silks are pasted on like cheap wallpaper; the jewels on the fan are furniture tacks; the skin is redone in Paris green; and two joke-shop flies have been added, one on the wall, one on a bare, green shoulder. Everyone wants to whisk them off or even swat them. Hence the glass.

In the case of *Painted on 21st Street*, artist Helen Frankenthaler added coffee grounds to the paint when she did the upper right-hand corner. Again, people would try to brush them off, or add something of their own if it weren't for the glass.

Cy Twombly's *August Notes from Rome* incorporates graffiti and many lumps and blotches. A glass cover bars viewers from adding their own scribbles or a wad of their own bubble gum. And Paul Sarkisian's *trompe-l'oeil* painting of newspapers is so convincing that viewers try to feel the texture, even turn the pages. Especially, since there's a headline announcing Elvis Presley's death and what appears to be a photograph of him.

It's just a painting, no kidding. And it requires a fence around it.

Confiscations That End Up
in the Smithsonian

Lawmen who nab things in the course of their duties often wind up with storage problems—and make friendly overtures to the Smithsonian.

What's Customs to do with giant sea-turtle shells? They're bought in the tropics by tourists who are taught a lesson at U.S. points of entry: it's illegal to import endangered sea-turtle products. The shells are tub-size, and not entirely stackable.

A truckload of 100 are sent to Natural History's vertebrate zoologist who's monitoring the life history of these creatures. He already has specimens of all the species, but not at every stage of development. He inspects the gift batch— of ridleys, greens, hawksbills—and sends off the discards and duplicates to schools and to other museums, keeping the shells he needs to fill in gaps in his collection.

Customs nabs orchid plants, too, carried home by travelers who lack entry permits. The Smithsonian welcomes the contraband plants to the nation's most extensive orchid collection, where each is logged in with an accession number and hung in the ranks of pots, stacked vertically in the greenhouse.

Six mint-condition slot machines, at American History, came from a Cleveland cache about to be wrecked by U.S. marshals. And drawers of opium pipes are remnants of raids from years back. A loaf of opium came with the pipes, but it was recently removed from the study collection. Curators got nervous about keeping it, even as a bit of history. The Treasury Department sent around an armored truck for the pickup.

—

The Homemade Leg

Visitors to the Museum of American History ask about it still, the artificial leg, handmade out of everyday materials, and worn by its maker for 15 years. Deroy Hill, a South Carolina farmer, had lost his leg in an accident. He outlined another one in steel, added chains, hinges, shims, and various scraps to make it fit in a boot, then strapped it on his hips. It weighed 20 pounds and worked fine from 1947 to 1962. Deroy kept right on with the farm chores and the cotton picking.

The Smithsonian got his homemade leg when he was finally fitted with a modern, scientific prosthetic limb. No one knows whether Deroy liked it as well as his old one. But when the loan period for the patchwork leg expired, someone wanted it back home.

—

Filming "The African Queen"

One of the most valuable collections given to the Museum of African Art was Eliot Elisofen's photographs, some 68,000 of them. He was a *LIFE* photographer who covered Africa for many years and collected its art, and his bequest helped get the little museum off the ground.

One of Elisofen's caption sheets, in the collection, is an account of the filming of *The African Queen* with Katharine Hepburn and Humphrey Bogart. And here, for the first time, are details of the hazards of filming in that location. Hepburn's broad-brimmed hat went limp in the humidity and had to be restarched daily. And her dress had to be re-dyed frequently. The blazing sun bleached it.

The Hidden Indian Treasure

It's been said that the Smithsonian discovered the American Indian. Until collectors and anthropologists from the Institution began ranging the West in the 19th century, full knowledge and appreciation of Indian culture simply didn't exist. As in other fields of research, spectacular Indian objects from the field have often gone on display. Except one.

Around 1841, Captain Charles Wilkes, whose Exploring Expedition provided hundreds of collections to the United States, ventured up California's Sacramento River and came back with an extraordinary Indian garment. It's a blanket of wild waterfowl feathers, as light and soft as a cloud, and extremely fragile. Maidu Indian women made these delicate objects and the men wore them as capes. The feathers overlapped, as they would on a bird—gray across the back, with black stripes that meet in front, and edged by bands of white and irridescent blue. The white came from Canada goose breasts; the blue from mallards and wood ducks.

By the end of the 19th century, no more of these marvelous garments could be found. Some 12 still exist. The Smithsonian's was on exhibit at the Patent Office, before the collections were turned over to the new Institution. As far as anyone knows, the feather cape wasn't displayed again until it reemerged for the 1985 celebration of the Wilkes expedition.

■

Mother Tusch's Wallpaper

Somewhere in the Air and Space Museum is a 185-foot-long strip of wallpaper, about two feet wide, peeled off the walls of a cottage in Berkeley, California. Why? Because it's covered with some 2,000 scrawled signatures—names like "Capt. Eddie Rickenbacker, Commanding Officer 94th Squadron. . . ." and "Floyd Bennett and his pal RE Byrd" and "H.H. Arnold, Commdg. U.S.A.A.F." and "J.H. Doolittle." It seems all the pioneers of American aviation are scribbled here somewhere.

The wallpaper belonged to Mary Tusch, a widow with two daughters. During World War I, aviation cadets were going through one of the army's first ground schools at the University of California, and she just happened to live across the street from that part of campus—close enough to hear reveille every morning.

One morning, the bugler made such a hash of it that Mary Tusch found out that he—and a lot of other cadets—had been shot down by the flu. She went to the infirmary with soup. She visited, wrote letters, boosted morale, and finally opened her house to the convalescents. They sang around the piano, ate home cooking, held dances, and talked end-lessly about this strange new business of flying.

"Mother" Tusch's cottage became known as "The Hangar." Cadets brought her their photographs when they shipped out to flight school. And one of them, on impulse, jumped on her sofa and signed his name high up on her wallpaper. It was new wallpaper, and she wasn't exactly overjoyed, but the boy simply said, "Too late." And of course all the others then followed suit. The wallpaper turned into a huge autograph book and the names proliferated: Billy Mitchell; Mason Patrick, C.O. of the old Air Service; Bert Balchen, who flew with Admiral Byrd; a German Luftwaffe pilot; Amelia Earhart; Ruth Law, the first woman to loop. Insignia, medals, maps, gloves, and helmets were added to the collection.

Hap Arnold roused the Smithsonian's interest and Paul E. Garber, first curator of aviation, went out to California. He collected Mother Tusch's wallpaper—and also one of her daughters for his wife.

—

The Tiny George Washington

Two engravings of George Washington are the smallest portraits at the National Portrait Gallery. They were done by an exiled Frenchman, Charles Balthazar-Julien Fevret de Saint-Memin. He also portrayed Lewis and Clark, Paul Revere, Elizabeth Seton, and Thomas Jefferson, whose daughter insisted that Saint-Memin do the miniature portrait because it was "what we have allways [sic] most wanted in our lives."

The artist first made large drawings by outlining his subjects' profiles with a physiognotrace, then reduced them to miniatures with a pantograph. The standard size was two-and-a-half inches, but the ones of Washington are about the size of a fingernail. They were intended to be set in rings.

Saint-Memin charged $25 for 12 likenesses of male sitters. Women cost more: $35.

—

What to Save for the Smithsonian

Sometimes there is a considerable gap between what people think the Smithsonian wants and what the Smithsonian actually *does* want. When women first entered the U.S. Naval Academy, a Smithsonian curator arranged, as a routine matter, that their uniforms should be saved for the Smithsonian collections. But when the Navy issued official underwear for the "female midshipmen," the curator caught the women by surprise. He asked them to save *that*, too.

Another curator accepted the offer of an elderly gentleman to come and look over the uniforms he had saved from the time of the Spanish-American War. There they were, laid out across a bed: dress uniforms that had been worn perhaps four times a year, beautifully cared for and in excellent condition.

"What about your fatigue uniforms?" the curator asked.

The old veteran waved a hand toward some packing boxes awaiting pickup by a charity.

The curator investigated, and found the work clothes that soldiers wear every day and quickly forget. *This* was the pay dirt for the Smithsonian.

Such a find more than made up for a dumb move earlier on the curator's part. In tidying his life, between his World War II military discharge and the start of his job at the museum, what had he done with his seven pairs of Army boots? Pitched them out!

—

Ray Guns
and Rocket Pistols—on Loan

Buck Rogers and his interplanetary rocketship was a special chapter in the story of man's dream to fly in space. And as the Air and Space Museum raced along toward its Bicentennial opening it had a gap where this chapter belonged.

Three fans of Buck Rogers came to the rescue. One was the son of Buck's originator. One was the father of an Air and Space curator. And one was a jet-propulsion scientist who'd read *Famous Funnies* as a tot and come early under the spell of teleporting between star systems.

By opening day the exhibit case was filled with Buck Rogers disintegrators and rocket pistols, solar scout badges and decoding rings, and balsa-wood rocketship model kits.

Other Buck Rogers fans press their noses to the glass—understanding why it is that the labels say "lent by" and not "gift of." (Astronaut Michael Collins's toothbrush from Apollo 11 has a lent-by label, too.) Some things a person has a hard time parting with.

▬

Red Horse
and the Little Bighorn

The Museum of Natural History is famous for the acres of shelves and cabinets and cases, away from the display area, where thousands upon thousands of items are stored. Here are beetles and bones, shells and stones. And in a big shallow drawer at the anthropology archives are 41 drawings. They tell the story of Custer's last stand, and they were done by a participant in that battle at the Little Bighorn in June 1876. He was a Miniconjou Sioux chief named Red Horse.

The chief recorded the battle five years after it was over. He used pen and colored pencils on great sheets of manila paper. He also narrated all that he saw and knew that hot day to a scholar of Indian sign languages, Col. Garrick Mallery. The colonel transcribed Red Horse's narrative four ways: first in diagrams, then by describing the hand gestures in great detail—the position of the fingers, the kind of movement of the hand, whether rapid or tremulous—then the text in the same word order as in the Indian language, and finally in flowing English.

According to these texts, Red Horse and four women were digging up wild turnips a short way from camp when "one of the women attracted my attention to a cloud of dust. . . . The soldiers were charging the camp. . . ."

The drawings show the battle raging. Bullets cross with arrows in mid-air; lances, clubs, and hatchets stab and bash. The warriors lean across the necks of their piebald ponies.

A wounded trooper hangs from his saddle by a leg. When the cavalry retreats, hoofprints are drawn, leading away from the Indians.

Red Horse spared no feelings. On his manila pages, blood spurts in red ink, dead horses pile up on the battlefield, soldiers are stripped, scalped, disemboweled, and have their limbs hacked off. Their flags and bugles are scattered around the bodies. And among the Indians leaving the scene are some carrying army carbines, some wearing cavalry uniforms.

Red Horse omits one historic figure. George A. Custer, known to the Indians as the Long-Haired-White-Man-Soldier-Chief, isn't identifiable. The trouble was he had cut his long blond hair before the battle.

The Smithsonian has a number of mementos of the Little Bighorn at the Museum of American History. There's a carbine, a ring, a McClellan saddle, a Smith and Wesson six-shooter. And there's a neck vertebra, identified as Caucasian. It has a metal arrowhead embedded in it.

—

The Twin Fetish
of Nigeria

Among the Yoruba people of Nigeria, one small piece of wooden sculpture appears frequently. Known as an *ere ibeji*, this small figure is so important to Yoruba culture that battalions of the little carvings stand in ranks on storage shelves at the Museum of African Art as back-ups to the ones on exhibit.

The Yorubas produce twins at the world's highest rate, and consider them sacred and lucky. The trouble is, the Yorubas also have a high rate of infant mortality. Many of the twins that are thought to bring good luck are born prematurely, and soon die. When that happens, an *ere ibeji* is carved. It is not a child's likeness—nor is it even childlike—but it does bear the scarification of the dead twin and is of the same sex. And always, it has the genitals of a young adult at the peak of physical perfection. The bereaved mother feeds the figure, and bathes and clothes it, along with the surviving twin.

That way, good fortune may linger in the household.

Wanted: False Mermaids

Some mammals at the Natural History Museum are known only through their skeletons collected in owl regurgitations; certain seaweeds have been found only where they were attached to a turtle shell or growing in a bucket or a watering-trough. One rare fossil "pineapple" was found doing service in a rock garden. Collector Robert Kennicott in the 1860s sent back from Alaska not only caribou but the grubs he found in a caribou nose.

Early annual reports of the Smithsonian used to list the Secretary's wishes under "Principal Desiderata," so the public would know that Florida pouched rats were welcome (in 1854)—also gopher snakes, copperheads, saiamanders (for the capture of which the recommended bait was sweet potatoes).

Today, in a kind of link with the past, Natural History's Naturalist Center posts (along with notices of field trips for the amateur botanists who use the Center's collections, library, and equipment) a list of specimens the Center needs for its herbarium of Washington-area plants: WANTED: DEAD OR ALIVE: Umbrella Wort, Water Wort, specimens from the False Mermaid family. . . .

—

A Helping Hand
for the Foucault Pendulum

People are apt to think that the Foucault Pendulum is some sort of perpetual motion machine. It isn't. Though the swing of that 240-pound brass bob seems as dependable as the rotation of the earth—which it illustrates—it requires complicated electronic assistance to keep it going and more than a bit of human muscle to get it started if it stops.

The pendulum hangs at the end of a thin, strong cable that passes through a well in the Museum of American History from the fifth to the first floor. It swings in a straight line, passing through the exact center of the circle set in the floor. Every 24 minutes it knocks over one of the red pegs that stand around the circumference of the circle. Since the pendulum swings straight, the floor must rotate in order to move a new peg into the path of the bob. And so it does: the floor rotates, the building rotates, the city of Washington rotates—the earth rotates.

But because of air friction, that great bob would slow and stop if it didn't get some help. This comes from a doughnut-shaped electromagnet high up in the well, which gives the pendulum a small kick on each outward swing to keep it going.

Even so, the Foucault Pendulum may slow and stop because the building vibrates or the power fluctuates or some other ''glitch'' destroys the even swing. Then a human starter, wearing white gloves to keep the brass shiny, must pull that heavy bob beyond the line of pegs and let it go exactly right, without a spin, so that it passes through the center of the circle. Sometimes he has to give it a few extra shoves—as you do to a child on a swing—to get it moving right.

"Nowadays," says the starter, "we don't even stop the pendulum for the night. The rule is: if it works, don't fix it!"

Broken Pots as Art

In a Freer Gallery storeroom are collections of "mends" (repaired pottery) and "wasters" (pottery that didn't come out right when it was made). There's a teabowl by the famous

Japanese potter Koetsu, which shows not only tea stains from 300 years of use, but mended cracks. These have been made into a kind of decoration, the repairs carried out with lacquer mixed with pigments so that the cracks seem patched with gold and silver and cinnabar red. And the lacquer, used like glue, was burnished. A cracked teabowl is similarly mended with a decor of tiny gold cherry blossoms on the surface.

Chinese porcelains, too, show off their long-ago repair jobs. Hand-wrought iron staples have been clamped into holes drilled on either side of a crack. Even on Neolithic earthenware at the Freer, the same method was used, but the holes were drilled with sticks and sand, and the staples were wet leather that shrank as it dried.

Potters have always made mistakes, occasionally, but their "wasters" haven't always been stored away in a museum so that interested viewers can look them over. At the Freer there's a 12th-century Chinese bowl of celadon blue—Chun ware—that got fused to its "sagger," the crocklike container that held it during the firing process and protected it from wood ash that would have spoiled its glaze. About 50 percent of ancient firing resulted in wasters like this.

Another piece of Chun ware is a beautiful little bowl, sky blue with a blush of red. It, too, stuck to its sagger just enough to crack on separation, and then it was mended with staples. Its maker must have liked it too much to pitch it out.

Oriental visitors to the Freer sometimes break into tears of happiness when allowed to see—even to hold—the mends and wasters. And working potters of every ethnic background agree that the collection of bungled jobs is not only an instructive but a consoling sight.

—

Jefferson's "Bible"

Thomas Jefferson's cut-and-paste "Bible" is a slim little book—short and precious, he called it—with just the passages he chose to keep. These he snipped from identical New Testaments and pasted onto blank leaves he then had bound. In retirement at Monticello, he read nightly from his homemade volume.

Cutting the Gospels didn't trouble Jefferson, for to him they were human documents and the Gospel writers—Matthew, Mark, Luke, and John—were "unlettered" men who frequently misunderstood the words of Jesus. The true words, said this confident cutter, were "as easily distinguished as diamonds from a dunghill." Jefferson also referred to his editorial work as "paring off the amphibologisms."

Gone from the Gospel according to Jefferson are all the miracles of healing and walking on water and feeding multitudes. Gone the voices of angels and the resurrection.

Most of Matthew's report of the Sermon on the Mount remains. All the "blesseds"—"blessed are the meek . . ."—

but the Sage of Monticello cut Matthew's concluding verse: "Be ye, therefore, perfect" and substituted from Luke, "Be ye, therefore, merciful. . . ."

In his youth, Jefferson had renounced the Anglican Church. Later, he considered himself again a Christian. Yet he never made his religious beliefs public or defended himself during presidential campaigns when he was bitterly attacked as an atheist.

Jefferson's first cut-version was a book of 45 pages. It was too hastily done, he later said—the work of a few evenings when he was distracted by other duties (that is, the Presidency). The Smithsonian has the second "Bible"— of 88 pages—done probably in 1819. Here Jefferson placed in columns, side by side, Greek, Latin, French, and English texts, shredding eight New Testaments in the process.

It was the find of two of the curiously mutilated volumes (the English-language ones, now also at Smithsonian) that led to the search, many years after Jefferson's death, for the "Bible" itself. The man who tracked it down and bought it from a Jefferson great-great-granddaughter locked up the book for protection while he was the Smithsonian's librarian—and carried the key in his vest pocket at all times. In recent years, the cut-and-paste book made a rare appearance in an exhibit on "Jefferson as Scientist."

Mural Makes
Bomber Crew Live Again

People entering the World War II gallery at the National Air and Space Museum are confronted by an epic painting. It's the mural by Keith Ferris: a huge B-17 flying straight at the viewer while others of its squadron hold formation below it. All spew their contrails against the cobalt sky of high altitude. Flak bursts pepper the background, and a German fighter begins its turn for an attack.

Artist Ferris set out to portray an exact moment on one plane's particular mission, and he dug through records until he found what suited him. He wanted a veteran B-17G with the paint showing wear, with interesting squadron and group markings, with a name and artwork in reasonable taste (many were pretty raunchy in those days when 50 percent casualties were not unusual). He wanted to paint the height of 8th Air Force activity—July to December, 1944. He wanted a combination of good weather, contrails, bursting flak, and enemy fighters.

Ferris came up with his plane, *Thunderbird*, on its return from its 72d mission, a raid on Wiesbaden on August 15, 1944. The time: 11:45, just 17 minutes after the bombs fell away and the great ships wheeled around toward home. They still have a long way to go, and the eyes of pilot and copilot, visible above their oxygen masks, show it.

Those eyes have added a new dimension to the mural. Ferris painted them with the same care as he did every patch, every bit of flaked-away paint, every mission marker on the plane (someone said that if there was a rivet on the plane, it's in the painting). He used photographs of *Thunderbird's* crew at the time. When a woman entered the gallery with her son in 1976 and saw the great B-17 coming at her, she started to say, "That looks like the plane your father flew." Instead, she said, "The copilot looks like your father."

They checked it out—and it was! Later, the widow and son of the pilot came to look at the mural; also the father of the bombardier. And the radio-gunner himself has shown up. He's the only survivor of that crew. Nine days after this mission, the rest were killed, flying a different plane.

Ferris painted in one small inaccuracy. He adorned the handle of the bombsight, which is shaped like a beer can, with the label of a brand of beer. It was the beer he happened to be enjoying as he got to that part. The Air and Space people, of course, would have made him paint it out if they'd noticed. Fortunately, perhaps, they didn't.

—

The Curator Who
Was the Janitor—or Vice Versa

John Varden was his name, and the early Smithsonian was his business. When the first collections were moved into the newly finished Castle in 1857, Varden packed and unpacked them and set up exhibits. He called the place "the Smithson Building," and he kept a careful log of the work hours he put in there, the chores he did, the weather, his church attendance (regular), and the state of his bowels (irregular). "Unwell all day with the Dioreah," he would note, along with a list of such tasks as unpacking skins and eggs, cleaning deer heads, polishing the glass over mummies, making storage trays, and putting his "plains and saws in order." Some spoke of him as curator; others as Smithsonian janitor. He seems to have been a bit of both.

Though Varden had little education and was a free soul when it came to spelling, he had, for five years, owned the first museum in the city of Washington—"a rational place for amusement." He then went to the Patent Office as assistant curator of collections. When the items were transferred to the Smithsonian, Varden came along, too.

His diary indicates the perpetual museum worry about deterioration. He went to some lengths to document his caretaking procedures so he wouldn't catch it if something went wrong: "Note: the Shawls, Carpet and Horse Covers Much motheaten when Put into my care . . . and I have had much trouble to keep them having scalded them three times with a strong solution of arsenic." Finding the textiles beyond his "power to Save," Varden writes, "I therefore made this Memorandum to prevent any blame being attached to me in the future."

Still, the curator-janitor pulled one hair-raising stunt with one of the most historic and incalculably valuable collections in the Institution. His entry for Thursday, October 14, 1858, says he got to the museum "at 7½ Cloudy and Cold, and like for Rain. Went to work again among the Japan and China Specimens brought home by Com. Perry as Presents to President Pierce, took some cuttings from the many Duplicate peices of Silk, for hankersheifs for wiping Spesimens with having worn out my own in the Service. . . . Left . . . at 5 P.M. fine Afternoon and had a glorious time at the Church."

—

Pigface—the Zoo's Oldest Inhabitant

The oldest inhabitant of the National Zoological Park is Pigface. No, that's not a homely keeper. Pigface is an African freshwater soft-shelled turtle at the Reptile House, and he's been at the Zoo longer than any keeper—longer than any Zoo employee at all.

The Firestone Expedition to Africa collected Pigface in 1937, when he was about two feet in diameter. Now he's added another foot in breadth, but that doesn't mean that he's exactly robust in appearance. Always flat and flabby, Pigface now looks like a slab of rubber, pushing itself around its deep-water tank with lazy waves of its flipper feet.

—

The Big Blaze

Three hundred portraits of Indians went up in flames one wintry afternoon in 1865. They had hung in a gallery on the second floor of the Smithsonian Castle and had been prized by sightseers, many of them Indians, who toured Washington in those days as delegates to their Great Father, the President.

The great Smithsonian fire should never have happened. The red sandstone building—the first in Washington to have steel beams—was constructed of fireproof materials, all except for its wood rafters. It had hoses and barrels of water in the right strategic places. And watchmen making rounds.

But in a week that was extremely cold, workmen had blundered. Installing a stove in the Indian gallery, they'd inserted the flue into what looked like a chimney. Unfortunately, it wasn't. It was a ventilating shaft opening to the rafters. And when heat built up and sparks flew, the rafters caught on fire.

By all accounts there never was such an impressive blaze. Flames soared and hissed, whipped by easterly winds. They burst from the roof and mounted the towers. Down below, on the Mall (then called the Smithsonian Reservation), crowds watched—10,000, 20,000 strong. And many spectators, even as roof and towers fell, had to be held back from rushing in to rescue national treasures.

Lost that day were all but a few of the 150 Indian paintings by Charles Byrd King, who painted them in a Washington studio under government contract, and all but a few of the 150 Indian paintings by John Mix Stanley, who had traveled the Far West with military survey parties. (Today, the surviving canvasses are at the National Museum of American Art.) Stanley's entire collection—the pride of his life—had been on loan to the Smithsonian. He had wanted to sell it and Secretary Henry had wanted to buy. But Congress had never come up with the $19,000.

Ironically, a delegation from the University of Michigan was visiting the gallery the day of the fire to see about buying Stanley's paintings. Ironically too, George Catlin's canvases—a comparable record of Indian life—which had also been offered for sale to the Smithsonian, survived the fire by having rested—relatively safely—in the boiler room of a Philadelphia locomotive factory, whose owner had taken them in 1852 for paying off the artist's debts. (Congress hadn't come up with cash for the Catlins either.) The factory owner's widow some years later donated the paintings to the Smithsonian.

In addition to Indian portraits, the fire consumed personal belongings of founder James Smithson: a trunk full of his notes, a collection of his small specimens of minerals, some pairs of silver-plated candlesticks, salt cellars, his bread basket, reading shade, and vinegar cruet. Small remnants of a lifetime, in any case, but almost all that the Smithsonian had of its enigmatic benefactor.

Lost as well: scientific apparatus, including a lens that figured in Joseph Priestley's discovery of oxygen and sundry belongings of scientists who lived in the Castle, accepting lodgings in lieu of salary.

Paleontologist Fielding Bradford Meeks, who was to continue to live in the Castle—in all, 18 years—listed damages for the ruin of his bedstead, one partly worn frock coat, one pair of gum-elastic overshoes, and two pairs of socks.

Flames never reached Secretary Henry's apartments in the east wing. He was lucky, even the looter making off with his boots was caught in the act. Also spared from the fire was the library in the west wing and the entire museum portion of the building—the Great Hall of exhibitions directly beneath the Indian gallery. All the national relics— the presidential portraits and the myriad trophies, fish, flesh, and fowl, from decades of Western exploration—were saved.

Relief, of course, was great, though a crabby columnist writing in *Frank Leslie's Weekly* two weeks after the fire said the building was monstrously inappropriate and inconvenient anyway and he only hoped the damage to it was so extensive "as to render its entire demolition necessary."

Demolition, indeed! The Castle was briskly rebuilt. But not a nickel ever went to artist Stanley for his loss.

—

An Artist's Party—
on Canvas

At the Hirshhorn Museum is a strange three-dimensional painting (or perhaps sculpture) called *Loft on 26th Street*. It's the work of Red Grooms, a filmmaker as well as artist, and memorializes his studio apartment, which he lost when the building was torn down.

Grooms reproduced in miniature every plate and cup, put his cigarette pack where it would have been, showed the postcards tacked on the wall. Then, from cardboard, he cut out figures of his friends and peopled his flat with them. It seems a nice bohemian artists' party—people cooking and eating and dancing. Grooms himself slices cheese at the sink.

—

The Seeing-Eye Dog
in the Discovery Room

The Discovery Room is the second most asked-for place at the Museum of Natural History, right after the nearest rest room. This is where both adults and children, at the rate of 10,000 a month, can touch the exhibits, pull special items out of drawers for close study, and test themselves on identification of shells or bones or mounted birds.

Blind people love the place because the way they "see" is by touching, and here is a tactile feast for them. There are Braille labels, but they're not much used—except by those who don't need them. One blind woman went through the shell collection, correctly identifying every single one by touch, without resorting to Braille. The whole room watched her with growing admiration, trying not to infringe on her privacy, but silently cheering her on.

Dogs aren't allowed in Smithsonian museums unless they're K-9 guard or seeing-eye dogs. One of the latter led its mistress to the Discovery Room one weekend. While she reveled in her discoveries, her dog headed straight for a bleached bone and was settling down to afternoon tea when the docents intervened.

—

The Masterpiece of the Alley

It's called *The Throne of the Third Heaven of the Nations Millennium General Assembly*, and it's one of the most popular sculptures at the Museum of American Art. The artist was a night janitor in Washington, D.C., who worked on it for 14 years in a garage in an alley—a far cry from its present situation in a museum enclave where it greets visitors.

It's a huge piece of work, an assemblage of altars, crowns, wings, and other ornamental devices. Exactly 177 separate pieces, ranging from heavily adorned tables to simple wall hangings, symmetrically surround the throne itself. Everything is wrapped in silver and gold foil. The artist worked at it secretly, for it was his own private dream, this creation, and he didn't want his neighbors to laugh at it.

But people *did* learn of it, including a Washington cabbie. And when the artist died, and his landlord prepared to sweep the strange structure out of that garage, the cabbie alerted a *Washington Post* photographer. The resulting photograph stirred the juices of a Smithsonian museum official. So the Institution bowed toward the late janitor's talent and acquired his beloved work.

—

Judy Garland's Slippers

Some Smithsonian items are acquired only at great difficulty or expense or as the result of derring-do—hacked out of cliffs, or dived for, or dug for, or sifted for through elephant dung and such muck. Some just come to the lucky Institution all unexpectedly.

A pair of Judy Garland's ruby-colored sequinned slippers, from *The Wizard of Oz*, floated in over the rainbow from an anonymous donor. These, at American History, are the size 5's for the star to wear over socks, not the 4's for barefoot wear or a third pair for the understudy.

—

Thousands of
Strange Smithsonian Nests

A lot of people might say that when you've seen one bird's nest you've seen them all. The Smithsonian disagrees. It has some 10,000 nests stowed out of harm's way, guarded from mildew or rot or jostling. One is the nest of the long-tailed (oldsquaw) duck, sent to Spencer Baird, second Smithsonian Secretary, from Greenland in 1860. It's big as a shopping basket, a fragile-looking swirl of love grass, packed with down and moss, containing nine of the original ten eggs. Other nests, smaller, are attached to a tree branch, in old cigar boxes, in tin cans, in logs, in sections of mud-bank, in beards of moss, in a human skull (wrens did that).

Some nests are double-decked. One pair of yellow warblers made a five-decked nest, new accommodations topping the old ones year after year. A kingbird nest in the collection incorporates a snakeskin among the building materials. Still another nest substitutes cellophane. A huge raven's nest was apparently too big for the materials its builder had at hand. Running out of sticks, the raven used the rib bones of an elk.

In the collection are the three known nests of the rare Bachman's warbler, all found in South Carolina. Here, also, are 37 edible birds' nests, sent to the Smithsonian by a missionary to China. Swifts fashion them of their own saliva, and gourmets pay most handsomely for the soup they make.

The Unhousebroken Mannequin

After a display of space underwear was set up at the National Air and Space Museum, a strange thing was noticed by visitors. Right at the foot of the astronaut mannequin a small puddle formed on the floor. People glanced at it as they passed, then stopped and came back. "Couldn't be," they would murmur to each other. Children, naturally, were less tactful. It seemed to them that it certainly *could* be, and they thought it hilarious.

The mysterious puddle remained on exhibit for six months. Eventually it was mopped up and explained away as condensation. A lot of Smithsonian visitors aren't really sure, however.

Charles Freer and the Chinese Bandits

In storage at the Freer Gallery are 39 stones. They're river stones, rounded by abrasion, about fist-size, and each has its own rosewood base, carved just to fit it. Maybe they're intended as weights to hold open an Oriental scroll. But again, maybe these common stones are at the gallery for no other reason than that they reminded Charles Freer of a month he spent exploring caves in northwestern Honan, China—a month the millionaire art collector considered the high adventure of his life.

He set out on his journey in 1910 to explore (with the Smithsonian's sponsorship) a pass called Dragon's Gate at the gorge of the Yi River. Here the mountainsides are honey-combed with sixth-century grottoes carved out of limestone, and at that time these caves were all but unknown, even in China.

The expedition struggled across roadless wastes, through miles of mud, over bridgeless creeks swollen by rain, urging on pack mules and ponies, carrying Freer in a sedan chair or sometimes on the back of a coolie. He reported that when he asked his bearers to slow down, his "imperfect Chinese" inspired them to fresh bursts of speed. Reaching Dragon's Gate at last, the party set up house in a temple far above the river and proceeded to explore the caves.

Freer was overwhelmed by the cave art—Buddhas and goddesses, high-relief lotuses on every surface. "I should have to live more lives to grasp it," he wrote. Only the extreme physical effort of climbing the gorge kept him, he noted to a friend, from going mad with the beauty. That and the brigands.

These latter were a routine problem to the Chinese, and Freer at first thought the stories about banditry were exaggerated. The expedition guards didn't want him to cut openings in the paper wall by his bed for fear the lurking brigands would enter, but Freer cut them anyway. He wanted the fresh air and the view of mists and mountains. Then a Chinese official dropped by, a fine looking mandarin preceded by a bearer with a red umbrella on a tall pole and troops who continuously blew trumpets and fired blank cartridges to warn off the bandits. He took a look at the set-up in the temple and dispatched six more soldiers to double the guard. That gave Freer something to think about. He agreed to the precautions.

From then on, Freer's guard kept up a rattle of musketry every night. The story goes that one night, on request, the shooting stopped, and in the morning the soldiers revealed that they had quietly cut the throats of marauders. "My cook," wrote Freer, "sleeps with the new breadknife . . . the photographer never sleeps, my servant wept last night when the temple cat mewed outside, so if the brigands overpower the guard, I shall dive under my folding cot."

Floods forced the party to leave ahead of schedule. Freer gathered his photographs and rubbings of carvings and reluctantly packed them up. Also, 39 stones from the bed of the River Yi. Whatever the use they were put to, they would always remind him of that glorious sojourn, nicely spiced with danger, at the Dragon's Gate.

The "Good-for-Nothing" Collector

Edward Nelson was no anthropologist. He knew nothing about it. He was just a young Army officer in the Signal Corps with a taste for adventure. When stationed at a small trading post on the Bering Sea coast of Alaska, he was asked by Secretary Baird to explore unknown territory along the coast and the Yukon and Kuskokwim Rivers and send some Eskimo artifacts back to the Smithsonian.

Of course, he jumped at the chance. The result is a collection of some 10,000 items at the Museum of Natural History—the world's most complete catalog of the way Eskimos not only flourished, but even developed beautiful and sophisticated art in what seems a totally inhospitable environment.

Nelson spent some four years in the 1880s, traveling nearly 5,000 miles by dogsled and kayak, visiting homes, learning the Yupik language, attending ceremonies. He took photographs like an inspired tourist, kept journals, compiled a dictionary. He shipped everything he could get his hands on—from kayaks to fish-hooks—to the Smithsonian. And since he hadn't a clue about anthropology and hence no opinions of the cultural value of his items, Nelson collected a pure sampling of the way Eskimo life was when he saw it. The things he sent have since opened the eyes of scholars to the ingenuity of these people, the common sense of their artifacts, their inevitable use of decoration, often humorous, always enchanting.

The Smithsonian still honors Nelson as a master collector. But the Eskimos who became his friends had their own name for him: "The Man Who Buys Good-For-Nothing Things."

—

Dapper Ben Franklin

Scholars researching 18th-century clothing may persuade curators at the Museum of American History to give them a look at Ben Franklin's party clothes—a three-piece purple silk suit. It's too fragile to face the public on display, but it's still there—coat, waistcoat, and breeches lying flat, supported by acid-free tissues, in a muslin-lined drawer in a locked cabinet in a room where temperature and humidity are carefully controlled.

Fine tailoring and rows of silk-covered buttons help account for the generally dashing look of the ancient suit. It seems still to express Franklin's tastes. So does its shape. It has a splendid bulge at the midriff, irrefutable evidence of much socializing, many splendid dinners, unnumbered syllabubs.

—

Thomas Moran Goes West

Thomas Moran, the American artist whose enormous canvases of *The Chasm of the Colorado* and *The Grand Canyon of the Yellowstone* seem to take up an entire gallery at the Museum of American Art, was the quintessential tenderfoot when he first went west. Born in England and raised in the American East, Moran illustrated a *Scribner's Monthly* article about Yellowstone without ever having seen it. He drew it as though it were about a yard wide. Perhaps disturbed by his own guesswork, he wangled a berth as artist with a geological survey, borrowed money, and set off.

Moran was 34, and a frail-looking 110-pounder who had never slept a night in the open, never even ridden a horse. His good friend, the expedition photographer, reported that he looked "incapable of survival," and that on the first day out he borrowed a pillow and crammed it under him "to protect his spare anatomy from the hard lines of a McClellan saddle." His friend said he was a picturesque sight with his yellow beard, jauntily tilted sombrero, slung rifle—and an artist's portfolio under one arm.

Moran not only survived, he thrived. His daughter noted that he was proud of his toughening physique and of the fact that for the first time in years he could stomach breakfast, munching down rashers of bacon with the best of the wranglers. "To him all was grandeur, beauty, color, and light— nothing of man at all, but nature, virgin, unspoiled, and lovely."

His mighty paintings, grand in scale and extravagant in color, helped preserve Yellowstone as a national park. And Moran, who signed some of them with a cattlebrand "M" superimposed on a "T," became known among his trailmates as T. Yellowstone Moran.

—

How's Your Atlatl Elbow?

Henry Collins, Jr., an anthropologist at the Museum of Natural History, traveled extensively among the Eskimos and learned a great many things about them. Atlatls, for example. He not only found many of these spear-throwing devices, but saw them used.

As a passenger, back-to-back in a two-person kayak, Collins saw a seal surface and his Eskimo companion react instantly with a forearm flick that drove a spear into the momentary target. A normal throw would never have reached the seal in time. But the hunter's atlatl, a narrow board with finger holes and a groove for the spear shaft, added 20 inches to his forearm, so the spear snapped away, fast and true.

Back at the museum, Lawrence Angel, the Smithsonian's famous bone expert, noticed signs of a special sort of arthritis of the elbow in some 3,000-year-old skeletons from California. He wondered what would cause it—what sudden, stressful, repeated extension of the forearm alone. Then Collins came along and suggested that the source of the arthritis was the atlatl. Sure enough, Angel found the elbow condition showing up less frequently in skeletons of female Indians, or of males who hunted with bow and arrow.

So "atlatl elbow" was born. Angel described it as a glazing of the joints like the polished look of a worn engine bearing. Cartilage has gone, and bone-to-bone contact has scored the joint with grooves. Skeletons of coal miners show something of the same thing.

Angel suggested that baseball pitchers may have atlatl elbow, but Collins disagreed. Not pitchers, he said. Pitchers take time to wind up before they throw. But catchers might have the condition. The catcher has to throw to second base from a squatting position while he's wearing all that padding. And he has to throw instantly when the base runner hurtles across his vision, just as the hunter must drive his spear at the sudden swirl of a seal. Both use a lot of forearm for that peg.

The hunter has the help of an atlatl. It's not legal yet for the catcher.

—

Carnegie's
Wonderful Boiler Room

It isn't an exhibit, but people who want to look at the boiler room in the basement of the Cooper-Hewitt Museum in New York are generally allowed to do so. The museum is in the grand old Fifth Avenue residence of the fabulous financier Andrew Carnegie, who had it built to his specifications. It was to be, he said, "the most modest, plainest, roomiest house in New York," but he liked his comforts and apparently, like many Scots, harbored a passion for steam engines—especially the giants that drove the great ocean liners of the turn of the century. The result is perhaps the world's finest, cleanest, most dazzlingly impressive private boiler room.

Black furnace doors, polished to a sheen, contrast with spotless white tiles. Fixtures are all glittering brass. Gauges are big and readable. The coal car runs on rails that include a turntable so it can reach any burner from the bin. The systems for hot water and heat are all doubled in case something goes wrong.

Nothing goes wrong any more. Nothing, in fact, goes. Carnegie's beautiful old systems have been shut down in favor of modern heating devices. But the Smithsonian staff keeps the place bright and clean, as though always ready for a captain's inspection.

—

Abigail Adams's Cookbook

Abigail Adams's cookbook survives, minus its covers, in the political history storerooms at American History. Rummaging through its brittle pages is not permitted, but visible through top and bottom of the book's special Plexiglas container are pages 56 and 57 and the P portion of the index. Even such limited contact brings a whiff of Colonial cookery and an image of generously laden White House tables.

One recipe on view prescribes three pints of cream, 15 eggs, one "glafs of Sack and two Spoonfuls of Rofe Water" for making "a Custard that is fit." Pies listed in the index include pigeon, calf's head, Neat's Tongue, Lamb Stones, swan, turkey, trout, eel, lamprey. There's a choice under

Possets: Sack-butter or Lord Carlifle's. Under Poultry, an entry on how to cure chicks of the Pip, of Flux, and Loufinefs.

Puddings here run to plain baked, plain boiled, or Black, plus a listing that includes Bifket, apple, bread, rice, millet, marrow, Beggar's Quaking, D. of Buckingham's, Spread-Eagle.

—

The Wardian Case

On the balcony of the Arts and Industries Building, above the great steam engines of 1876, is an exhibit of what might be called indoor gardening. Here are ferneries and terrariums and combinations of terrarium and aquarium, all with flourishing plants varying in size from miniature mantelpiece displays to complete parlor gardens, one with a built-in fountain. The idea of enclosed gardening goes back to an early-19th century doctor, Nathaniel B. Ward. While trying to hatch a moth in a small glass chamber, Dr. Ward noticed that bluegrass had sprouted in the soil. He began designing glass cases for growing plants. This allowed exotic varieties to be carried on a ship's deck with plenty of sunlight and no killing salt spray. With these Wardian cases of various sizes and architectural styles, Victorians could fill their homes with lavish greenery, climbing and creeping, cascading and weeping.

Smithsonian horticulturist James Buckler frequently lectures about plants and often gives a nod to Dr. Ward's portable invention. But for months, Buckler had no Wardian case for his exhibits. Then he got a phone call from a lady who offered to donate her greenhouse to the Institution.

How big a greenhouse, Buckler wanted to know.

Not big at all, she told him. It was sitting on a table beside the telephone.

Buckler drove over immediately and came away with the Smithsonian's first Wardian case. Soon he had four "originals," all dating from the mid-19th century, and another made at the Institution by one of the gardeners. The cases may have a greenhouse shape or classic columns or a rustic look with miniature tree trunks supporting the glass. Rarest in our collection is a little church with a steeple.

Adventures of the
Original "Old Glory"

We use the nickname "Old Glory" for any American flag. But in the Museum of American History, in an alcove where the light is rather dim to preserve the colors, the original Old Glory is displayed. It's a huge flag, 10 by 20 feet; the blue field, with an anchor in the midst of the stars, is the size of a banquet table. And it looks in good shape, considering that it dates from 1824.

Even larger than the flag is its history. It was made in Salem, Massachusetts, for Captain William Driver, by his mother, his sisters and his girl friends, so he could fly it over his first command, the vessel *Charles Doggett*. Driver (a wonderful name for a sailing ship captain!) had run off to sea at 13 when he was an apprentice to a blacksmith. The smith's wife may have driven him to it when, on a Sunday morning, she dressed him in a ruffled shirt for Sunday School. He never made it to his class. Instead, he cut off the ruffles and scampered off to Salem harbor in time to sign on as cabin boy aboard the ship *China*, just casting off on a voyage.

Driver liked the life, and was good at it. He got command of *Charles Doggett* when he was 21. It carried his flag—which he called "old Glory"—to New Zealand on that first voyage, and he was gone a month short of two years. And the great banner, his "steadfast friend and protector," sailed with him twice around the world. He flew it at Pitcairn Island when he helped resettle survivors from the famous *Bounty* mutiny. And he flew it every Fourth of July, wherever he was.

Captain Driver retired to a home in Nashville, and Old Glory went into a camphorwood chest. It came out three times a year: on Independence Day, of course; on Washington's Birthday; and on Driver's own birthday, which happened to be St. Patrick's Day. He would fly it from a line that stretched from his attic window to a locust tree across the street. When his son, Henry Driver, was old enough, he got the job of shinning up the tree to reeve the line through a block lashed to the tree trunk.

In 1861 Tennessee went with the South, and the Captain's flag was threatened. Driver bundled Old Glory into the sewing room and got his wife and two daughters, Mary Jane and Dillie, to repair it. "It needs overhauling," he told them. They cut and trimmed and added ten new stars, bringing the total up to 34, and the captain then added his anchor in the middle of the new pattern.

One night Driver lugged the restored flag over to the home of his neighbor, another staunch Union man named Bailey. Together they folded it up; then the Bailey girls, Mary and Patience, sewed on covers and quilted it as a bed comforter. And after that, while war erupted around him, the captain hid the bundle in a wash kettle in his attic.

On February 25, 1862, the Yankees took Nashville. Driver went to the wharf to greet them and brought a squad from the Sixth Ohio back home with him to watch him and Mary

Jane rip open the seams of the comforter and unfold Old Glory. Then, with a military escort, the Captain and his sons marched to the State Capitol and hoisted the old flag to the dome and cheered it as it floated free.

That night a gale blew up, whipping the flag so savagely that Driver got worried about it and substituted another. Old Glory went back to its camphorwood chest. When the Sixth Ohio left town, the captain gave them the substitute flag, which was made of heavy French wool. Later, when it was stowed in a baggage wagon, army mules found it and ate it. The press reported the humiliating end of Old Glory.

But the real Old Glory stayed in its chest, and when Mary Jane went west in 1873, her father gave it to her at the station. They say a crowd gathered on the train when he began retelling his Old Glory stories, and the train pulled out with Driver on board. It had to be backed up again to let him off.

Old Glory marked the next Independence Day, spread out at Salmon River, Nevada. Next year it was at the Driver brothers' mining camp at Goose Creek, Nevada. When Dillie saw it in 1891, it looked old. The blue field was shredding, the stars and anchor were yellow. A few years later it was sewn onto sheeting, and in 1923, it was presented to President Harding. He gave it to the Smithsonian.

Old Glory finally went on exhibit in 1983. It had been covered, by then, in an envelope of silk net, strong and almost invisible, to protect it. It looks fine. William Driver would approve.

———

The Artist Who
Signed with a Butterfly

James McNeill Whistler was not exactly modest about his art. When he painted his famous portrait, *Rose and Grey: The Princess from the Land of Porcelain,* he expected it to "make a big hurrah" and earn him a thousand pounds. He signed it in the upper left with his full name and the date—1874—two inches high.

The sitter's father, the Greek consul general in London, didn't give Whistler even a small hurrah. He disliked Whistler's Oriental treatment of his daughter—draping her in a kimono—and wouldn't buy the painting. Another prospect offered to buy, but only if Whistler shrank his signature to a more practical size. Finally, Frederick Leyland, a wealthy businessman, bought the portrait. It became the centerpiece of his opulent Peacock Room (executed by Whistler), which is now the centerpiece of the Freer Gallery.

Whistler's dominating signature remains on the portrait. Moreover, the Peacock Room contains in its decor four butterflies—Whistler's stylized monogram. He worked out the little insect shape by combining J,M, and W, and he used it when the trade called for it. Whistler came to like it because it was dramatic and different, and he signed some of his letters "Butterfly." They say he even signed some checks with the device. But not one of these is to be found at the Freer, which has the world's finest collection of Whistler's work.

—

Another Butterfly Signature

There is a corner in the National Museum of American Art devoted to the gray, penetrating paintings of Romaine Brooks. She was an expatriate American in Capri when Charles Freer met her and urged her to see Whistler's work in England. She did. The experience gave her work nuances not unlike Whistler's, and also the subdued grays that spelled England in her mind. She won recognition in Paris, where she was called "the thief of souls."

Paris also accepted Romaine Brooks as a lesbian. For many years she lived with Natalie Clifford Barney, poet daughter of Alice Pike Barney, whose Washington studio house is a Smithsonian treasure. Her tortured early life (she wrote about it as *No Pleasant Memories*) affected her art, especially her drawings. They are fantasies done in wiry lines, elegant and fluid, seeming to fly in a fury of painful thoughts.

She signed her paintings with a bold black signature: "Romaine." But she signed those drawings with a butterfly cipher—with a chain—or maybe a rope—holding down the wing.

—

John Bull's Whistle

John Bull, the world's oldest operable steam locomotive, celebrated its 150th birthday in 1981 by chuffing along a stretch of track beside the Potomac, hauling a railroad carriage, vintage 1830s, filled with costumed guests. And the little engine charmed thousands of onlookers with its whistle, a brisk little *peep*.

Actually, John Bull has three whistles, each equally interesting to the engine's curator. He calls them all "original." One is a small commercial whistle that might have been picked off a shelf in a plumbing supply house in the

1870s. Presumably it was, and then fitted to J.B. to spruce it up for the Philadelphia Centennial Exposition in 1876, where it was on display. Another is much older—almost as old as the locomotive—and may have adorned it at the Columbia Exposition of 1893. It doesn't fit on the present steam dome.

The third does. It's medium-size, dates from the mid-19th century, and was dropped off at the Smithsonian by a proverbial little old lady who said it was from John Bull. The curator thinks it was removed when the engine was retired from regular work in the 1860s. No one knows how the little old lady got it.

—

The Arcane Art of Gilding

At the frames shop of the National Museum of American Art, gilders go through their paces, restoring gilt to picture frames. It's a strange old business with its own traditions and vocabulary and an amazing array of equipment that stretches back through the ages.

Consider: a sheet of gold leaf is 1/250,000th of an inch thick. To pick it up, gilders may first run the camel's hair "tip"—a wispy little brush—through their hair to generate some static electricity. The tip carries the gold leaf to the "cushion" where it's cut to shape and applied to the frame.

Many gilders use a sheet of ox intestine on which to beat gold leaf, because it's not sticky. You brush "brime," a kind of powder, onto it with an Arctic hare's foot, which has a tuft of hair in the center of the pad and is the best brush in the whole world for the job.

Some of the other brushes are mops, cairns, quills, and fitches, each with a special function. One, made of squirrel hair, is used only to pick up gold shavings ("skewings") and slip them into cracks in a frame as filling.

To repair all the intricate moldings of a frame, gilders make gesso of plaster and glue: sturgeon-bladder glue from Russia, maybe, or, as the Italians used to prefer, glue from the necks of winter-butchered goats. The Smithsonian gilders mostly get along with rabbit-skin glue. They use Dragon's Blood from Malaysia, a tree resin, to deepen color. And they polish their work with agate or wolf's tooth.

Oh, incidentally, the best solvent for cleaning a frame is sometimes saliva or urine.

—

Secretary Baird's Remarkable Desk

Upstairs in the Museum of Natural History, in a warren of paleontology offices, is a monumental Victorian desk with

110 pigeonholes and shelves and drawers, all locked by one key. No one uses it, but it's not roped off with a plaque to tell people about it, either. It's just there, perhaps as a gentle reminder to passing staff scientists that once there was a man who kept it busy, using every one of its features—the opening wings, the glass letter box, the dropleaf with green felt lining, all those pigeon holes.

For the desk belonged to Spencer Fullerton Baird, second Secretary of the Smithsonian, a massive, carelessly dressed, lumbering giant. Baird's capacity for work was in direct ratio to his size. From 1850 until his death in 1887, he built the Smithsonian's collections—and its reputation in natural history—all the while finding snatches of time to write huge scientific tomes and hundreds of warmly personal, detailed letters to his collectors in the field.

He needed that desk because he needed all the room he could get for working and filing. And though he watched Smithsonian expenditures with a keen eye, he finally took the plunge and ordered the Wooton patent secretary, a high Victorian status symbol and the finest desk he could buy. He did enough work to strain the capabilities of two such as this.

Secretary Baird ordered just the standard model, of course. Not the Extra or the Superior. No frills.

■

Owls in the Castle

During the 1960s, the Castle's interior was gradually restored to the elegant Victorian style that fits James Renwick's architecture. Among other furnishings that were moved in to carry out the theme were some barn owls. Long ago owls used to live in an empty tower room, so the Smithsonian put them back. While the birds (provided by the National Zoo) were establishing residence, the Castle's curator climbed five sets of ladders five days a week to deliver their favorite food—rats. A deputy assistant secretary of state, an owl buff, took over on weekends.

For some months, the owls could be seen swooping in

and out of their open window. Then, despite all that pampering, all those hand-served meals, they took off to see the real world.

—

The Secretary Who Mined a Mountain and Found the Ancient Past

In the fall of 1909, at the close of a season's rock hunt, near Kicking Horse River Pass in British Columbia, Charles Doolittle Walcott, fourth Secretary of the Smithsonian and a noted paleontologist, was leading his heavily laden pack train toward a railhead. He dismounted to cast aside a slab of rock. It was smooth shale and he may have thought a horse might stumble or slip on it.

Ever the scientist, Dr. Walcott tapped the rock with his hammer. It split, and he saw exposed the images of life forms from the sea. They were perfectly preserved as a kind of carbon film—glossy black against the matte black of the shale.

Dr. Walcott was famous for his knowledge of the Cambrian period—the oldest period that produces fossils—from 530 million years ago. It was to explore this period in geology and paleontology that he had gone to Canada. He recognized instantly that he had found Cambrian fossils—but totally different from what had been known. These were soft-bellied, of a kind almost never before seen. And here, black on black, they were perfectly revealed.

Walcott, who was a hard man to excite, admitted later that the sight stirred his juices. He immediately scouted the mountainside to see where the slab had fallen from. About 750 feet above the trail, he found a seven-foot seam, tapering at the ends. He had to return to his duties at the Smithsonian Castle, but for five succeeding summers he returned to the Burgess Shale and quarried it by hand. He did his own blasting. He picked and sledged and scrabbled his way along the seam of fossils, dismantling the overhang as he went. He carried the slabs down from his 7,000-foot ''dig'' in his knapsack.

Today, Wolcott's treasure fills a 40-foot rank of cabinets, six feet high, at the Museum of Natural History. There are 60,000 specimens, representing many new species with myriad adaptations for life on the sea floor of Cambrian times. His find is in every textbook of fossils, though at first the scientific community of Europe thought this find must be some sort of American hoax.

In the 1960s a party of scientists found the site of Walcott's quarrying by helicopter and searched for specimens he might have overlooked. They found very few, and those were from the slabs of shale that Walcott had used to support his tent platform.

■

George and Martha

The most valuable paintings at the National Portrait Gallery are the famous unfinished "George" and "Martha." They're the portraits that the Smithsonian bought from the Boston Atheneum on condition that Boston would still share them. The Smithsonian gallery director who made this deal says that he's known in New England as the Boston Strangler, and takes a lot of flak in Washington, too. But the arrangement stands: three years in Boston, three in Washington.

In the paintings, Martha wears a mobcap and George wears his dollar bill look. Gilbert Stuart did them from life, on commission from Martha Washington. She never got them. Stuart kept the portraits with their bare canvas backgrounds, to serve as studies for future works. After all, a painting of Washington was a sure-fire hit back when the presidency was a brand-new concept.

The fact is, Stuart often started things he never finished. He used to get half his fee in advance, then if he didn't finish the work, he still had a profit. Pretty sharp, for an artist.

Alan Shepard's
Useless Parachute

Freedom 7 is the name of the little one-man capsule in the Air and Space Museum in which an American first traveled in the barely known realm of space. On May 5, 1961, astronaut Alan Shepard squeezed into this cramped little man-trap and was blasted into a 15-minute suborbital flight beyond the atmosphere and then back again.

By the right hand of the mannequin that now sits in Shepard's cockpit is a green packet that contains a parachute—perhaps the world's most useless parachute. Upon his return, Shepard said that all hand movements were difficult in his wedged-in, strapped-down position. Also, the Mercury spacecraft had no ejection system. So, if something had gone wrong on his flight, he would have had to attach that chute somehow to his chest, then remove the craft's instrument panels and open two hatches. Then climb out and jump.

The procedures would have taken five minutes—a third of the entire flight time.

Obviously, the parachute was put in there to make some people feel easier in their minds. But not the pilot. Shepard said he'd just as soon have done without it.

—

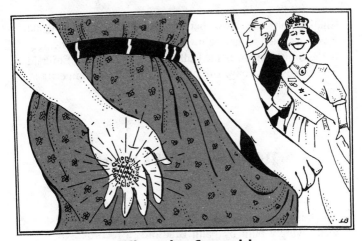

When the Emerald
Bowed to the Queen

In the Hall of Gems, not far from the Hope Diamond, there is a ring with a huge emerald, sparkling clear and green. The stone is nearly 38 carats—about as big as a gem could be and still fit on a ring—and is said to have been one of a set of earrings worn by Cleopatra. More recently, it belonged to Mrs. O. Roy Chalk, wife of a Washington financier.

During a state visit to Washington by Queen Elizabeth II, Mrs. Chalk wore her jewel to a royal reception at the White House. But she soon realized that she was putting the Queen's jewelry to shame. Quickly and tactfully, Mrs.

Chalk pivoted the ring on her finger so that the great emerald was concealed in her palm. Soon after, she gave the ring to the Smithsonian. In the Hall of Gems, the Chalk Emerald still comes on strong. But now it's got lots of competition.

—

TLC for Peter Doll's House

The huge dolls' house at the Museum of American History was lovingly built by Faith Bradford, a records expert at the Library of Congress. It tells the story of a family: Peter Doll, his wife Rose (née Washington), 10 children (it's a turn-of-the-century family), and visiting grandparents. The household includes a butler and a maid. There are pets—rabbits, a bulldog, white rats.

Faith Bradford put a lot of herself into the house—so much so that after turning it over to the Smithsonian, she couldn't quite let go of the family she had created. She used to show up twice a year with an artist's brush to dust every one of the Dolls' 2,000 belongings, and in between dustings, she'd come just to look or to give impromptu "tours" to interested visitors—provided, of course, that they were not wearing shorts, which she abhorred in public buildings. She'd point out the photo of her own cat, Mr. Bittenger, on the day nursery wall, and the fine clutter of furnishings in the attic, stored there because they were out of date or outgrown or broken.

Also, she invariably would get the Christmas wreath and the decorations out of attic storage and put them up when the Yule season rolled around.

Faith Bradford is gone. But the Smithsonian still makes sure that the wreaths are up, every Christmas. (The aim is to pack them away again soon after the Superbowl, though once the job wasn't done until the Fourth of July.)

—

Whale Skull Travail

The 19-foot whale skull at Natural History looks clean and white and innocently in place over the Dynamics of Evolution Hall. So no one guesses the travail that went into getting it there. On June 1, 1903, a 61-ton sulphur-bottom whale was brought in to Balena, a whaling station off the coast of Newfoundland, and a Smithsonian field man, Fred Lucas, claimed its head. Lucas had been waiting for a big carcass to be towed in by the whalers and he was sick of wading around in blubber and blood. Though this whale was a shade shorter than he wanted, it was close enough.

So Lucas had a whale's head on a Newfoundland dock. Now what? He tried to raise the snout and broke his lever—

a three-by-eight timber. It took two hours with two steam winches just to turn the head over. Then he had to ship it. That meant making a packing box as big as a room, braced like a railroad bridge. The crate weighed four tons and exactly fit inside a boxcar. The skull, with "some little meat and membrane" left on to pad it, was winched into it. There's no report on what the smell was like.

When the Natural History building opened in 1912, the skull wasn't in it. It didn't go on display for another 65 years, and by then it was pretty grimy, had been banged around by a forklift, and finally fractured. Presumably, however, it had stopped smelling. Smithsonian specialists glued pieces back together, strengthened the bones with steel rods covered with lengths of pipe, and hoisted the skull into place to look as though it had always been there.

—

A World in Boxes

An attic within an attic, at the Museum of American Art, is the collection of trinkets and vintage ephemera saved by one artist—his pingpong balls, keychains and jacks; his film stills and 19th-century sheet music; tins labeled "owls, ETC, fungi"; bottles of pencil shavings and glitter; and shoeboxes marked "Jetsam" and "Flotsam" and "Flotsam and Jetsam."

Eminent sculptor Joseph Cornell squirreled away the lot. His sculptures (on view at American Art and the Hirshhorn) are boxes—made of wood with glass panes—in which he fashioned a compelling dream world from his odd collections.

Cornell was a kind of homemade American surrealist. He lived on Utopia Parkway in Flushing, New York, and European artists made pilgrimages to meet him. But he, like poet Emily Dickinson, with whom he felt a kinship, was an armchair traveler. He rarely went anywhere except to Manhattan to comb second-hand bookstores, penny arcades, and novelty shops (he's been called the dimestore connoisseur) or to nearby beaches—to pick up shells, bits of glass, cork, driftwood.

When Cornell died, in 1972, his stockpiled source materials came to the museum. And all the optical toys and the quantities of bird cut-outs, perches, eggs, feathers, and nests were filled in 124 hefty cartons, along with the fat dossiers prepared by the artist on Celestial Navigation and on Celebrities—his admired movie stars and ballerinas. (Standing at the stage door with seamstress scissors, Cornell cut snippets of tulle and feather from the costumes of Tamara Toumanova for a sculpture box in her honor.)

Now scholars, schoolchildren, and artists visit the Joseph Cornell Study Center to ponder the feathers and pencil shavings and nests as clues to a complex inner life. The *New York Times* obituary called Cornell a "man who thought everything could be used in a lifetime." He had a lot in common with the Smithsonian.

■

Lindbergh's Letter
to Collins

Michael Collins, first director of the new National Air and Space Museum, was the astronaut who orbited the moon alone in the Apollo 11 spacecraft *Columbia* while his companions, Neil Armstrong and ''Buzz'' Aldrin, landed on the lunar surface. Collins later received a letter from Charles A. Lindbergh, who like most of the ''greats'' of aviation had watched the blast-off from Cape Canaveral and monitored the tremendous achievement.

In his letter Lindbergh, remembering his own epochal 33-and-a-half-hour solo flight from New York to Paris, touched on the the ''quality of aloneness that those who have not experienced it cannot know—to be alone and then to return to one's fellow men once more. . . . As for me, in some ways I felt closer to you in orbit than to your fellow astronauts.''

—

Teddy Roosevelt's Moose Heads

Theodore Roosevelt sent so many animals—skins, skulls, carcasses—to the Smithsonian that a newspaper cartoon once showed the Castle all but buried under crates of specimens bearing his name. But he didn't send his stuffed moose heads. Florence Harding, the rather formidable wife of President Warren G. Harding, did, after finding them still occupying the White House.

"I told Warren G. I was sending them to a cleaner," she later explained. "But they are *not* coming back. They smelled something fierce."

M*A*S*H Is a Smash

M*A*S*H had a long run on television, 11 years of doctors and nurses at the Korean front patching up fighting men to fight again. When the series ended in 1983, someone at American History thought to get a memento. He asked for a stethoscope. And he wound up with the operating room and the officers' tent, nicknamed the Swamp, plus the services of a set dresser who came with the gift to arrange all 2,000 items in the museum just as if cameras would roll again. When the stars checked the place out, they said it was as cluttered and cramped as it ought to be. And surgeon Hawkeye remarked, "Gee, Beej," to his sidekick B.J., "did you ever expect the Swamp to wind up at the Smithsonian!"

The Smithsonian never expected its M*A*S*H to be the hit it was, breaking all attendance records in its 19 months, with crowds milling around mornings before the doors opened and extra guards having to be laid on and a system of passes, too, to avoid five-hour waits in line.

The response surprised everyone. The museum's M*A*S*H (Mobile Army Surgical Hospital) was make-believe, at least twice removed from war's reality. It was based on a zany, irreverent TV sit-com based on a movie based on a book. And a row of studio lights hung above the operating room lights to show it.

Yet elements of it were as real as the crowd's affections. The Swamp's furnishings were Army-issue or period-Sears checked by the catalog. Operating room gear was authentic for the '50s. So were the uniforms. The dress of cheerful cross-dresser Corporal Klinger even had a double pedigree, having been worn earlier by Ginger Rogers. Boots were the exception. There weren't enough black boots from Korean war times to go around, so the cast wore Vietnam-era brown boots.

A fat folder of letters at the museum dates from the death in the series of popular commanding officer Henry Blake. When Blake, homeward-bound to Illinois, was shot down over the Sea of Japan, letters poured into the studio. They came from grandparents, working people, whole classrooms of fifth grade children and their teachers, asking, Why, why why? Why kill Blake? The script writers were surely clods, idiots, Sadistic Crackpots. They were cruel. They were SICK. Many letters contained threats or enclosed complex scenarios for a resurrection.

Only a few of the correspondents said they appreciated the message. War doesn't just kill the extras. War kills people you love.

Letters posted in the exhibit slowed down the lines snaking single-file past Hawkeye's tabletop martini still and nurse Hot Lips Houlihan's clipboard. People stopped to read— and it took them half an hour to walk a few short yards.

■

How the Bible Became
a Quilt

In the Museum of American History, visitors always pause before a wonderfully colorful cotton-calico quilt. Its squares allude to Biblical events, but they're different from what people expect. The serpent in the Garden of Eden, for example, has feet, and the other creatures around it—elephant, camel, ostrich, leviathan—have none.

Harriet Powers, who made the quilt, was born a slave. She first showed the quilt at the Cotton Fair of Athens, Georgia, in 1886. When a school teacher, Jennie Smith, wanted to buy it, Harriet Powers said it wasn't for sale at any price. But five years later, Mrs. Powers showed up at the teacher's house in an oxcart driven by her husband. She carried the quilt in a flour sack, inside a crocus bag. She told Miss Smith she could have it for $10.

Times were hard, and Miss Smith could only afford five.

Times were very hard, in fact, and Mrs. Powers accepted. But often she returned to look at her quilt and tell why she had made the squares the way she did. The feet on the serpent allowed it to "get around" Man. And Satan is surrounded by six discs and carries a seventh: These are the seven stars.

There are three spheres above the cross. The black one, said Harriet Powers, is the darkness that came over the world at the time of the crucifixion; the white one signifies the Lord's acceptance; the red one is the moon turning to blood.

Thirty pieces of silver surround Judas; the thirty-first disc in that square, bigger than the others, is "the star that appeared in 1886 for the first time in 300 years."

Finally, the Last Supper is shy five apostles. Why? Because Harriet Powers simply ran out of space.

—

"The Old Man Mad About Painting"

A Japanese scroll at the Freer is called *Miscellaneous Sketches* and is signed "The Old Man Mad About Painting." The artist was the famous Hokusai, who used some 50 pseudonyms. He once wrote: "I am dissatisfied with everything which I produced before the age of 70. It was at the age of 73 that I nearly mastered the real nature and form of birds, fish, plants, etc. Consequently, at the age of 80, I shall have got to the bottom of things . . . and at the age of 110 every dot and every line from my brush will be alive."

The *Miscellaneous Sketches* scroll is about 30 feet long and shows such vignettes as a snowscape, maple leaves floating on rippled water, bamboo leaves separating the filets of a mackerel, and a pack of red foxes racing over cracked ice. And in very small characters, alongside that odd signature, is the artist's reminder—he is "80 years old."

The Authors

Edwards Park is well known from his columns in *Smith-sonian* magazine and his mammoth *Treasures of the Smith-sonian*. Peggy Thomson has written about the Institution in numerous magazine and newspaper articles as well as in her books *Museum People* and *Auks, Rocks and the Odd Dinosaur*.

—